Christopher Columbus:
The Catholic Discovery of America

John A. Hardon, S.J.

Eternal Life

Imprimi Potest: Very Reverend Timothy P. Kesicki, S.J.
Provincial Superior
Chicago and Detroit Provinces, Society of Jesus

Christopher Columbus:
The Catholic Discovery of America
John A. Hardon, S.J.

© Inter Mirifica February 11, 2012
ISBN: 978-1-931101-04-2

Printed in the United States of America
By Eternal Life ®

ETERNAL LIFE ®
902 W STEPHEN FOSTER AVENUE
BARDSTOWN, KY 40004 USA
800-842-2871
www.lifeeternal.org

Cover photo source: dreamstime.com

FOREWORD

Christopher Columbus
As Missionary Apostle of the New World

Readers are indebted to Eternal Life for this important volume, *Christopher Columbus: the Catholic Discovery of America* by the Servant of God Fr. John Hardon, S.J., which contains the actual lectures given by the distinguished theologian on one of the most extraordinary figures in Western history. Secular historians have noted how this great explorer's success in discovering a New World and who was convinced until his death in 1506 that he had visited the outlying lands of Asia, was to profoundly affect every important aspect of later European and American history. In the words of one historian *"Vain, boastful, arrogant and deceitful he certainly was, and in his last years highly visionary; yet his tenacity, courage, hardihood, and independence indicate a man of heroic stature. His mistakes and defects of his character should not obscure the greatness of his achievement."* (Prof. Curtis P. Nettles, "The Roots of American Civilization", 1947). For Fr. Hardon, this standard historical interpretation of Columbus' life and achievement found in biographers and in the several thousand books written about Columbus fails to explain why it was Columbus who discovered America. *"They ask and they do not have the answer."* Why was it not the wealthy Chinese or the aggressive and expanding Muslim Arabs who had extensive knowledge of astronomy? And why the central role of Spain? It is the saintly Queen Isabella of Spain who provides the answer: *"She saw with God's grace, in Christopher Columbus the man destined by God to open a new world to the Gospel of Jesus Christ."*

It is with spiritual insight into God's plan of salvation and the workings of Providence that our Jesuit theologian examines Columbus' life and writings to discover what secular historians and others hostile to the Catholic Church have utterly failed to grasp: namely, that Columbus *"was the instrument of extraordinary grace...He was the destined herald of the true faith to half the human race."* A zealous and militant Catholic with a crusader's spirit, he had deep faith in the divinity of Christ, profound devotion to the Blessed Virgin and love of the Holy Eucharist. But he was *"no visionary"*. His remarkable work, "Book of Prophecies", constituted a *"full-scale study of the Messianic prophecies of the Old Law and the teaching of Christ about the duty to proclaim the Gospel to all nations."* Fascinating excerpts from this primary historical source reveal the depth of Columbus' faith and *"what may be called a mystical understanding of God's will for the world"*. That included his own mission as a specially chosen servant of God to discover what we now know as the Western Hemisphere and, above all, to convert its peoples to Jesus Christ and His Catholic Church. Fr. Hardon's research confirms that Columbus' dominant motive for sailing across uncharted seas was not economic and commercial, the search for wealth, or to bask in human glory but rather apostolic, *"to extend the Kingdom of Christ to pagan nations who had never had the Gospel preached to them."* It was this Admiral of the Ocean Seas who manifestly sowed the seed for the "avalanche of conversions" in Central and South America. Over eight million Aztec Indians in Mexico were to embrace Catholic Christianity on a scale of evangelization that had *"no equal in recorded Catholic history."* There are inspiring pages on the role of Our Lady of Guadalupe in the astonishing conversion of further millions in Latin America.

Fr. Hardon takes note of those in the English-speaking world who have been virulent critics of Christopher Columbus and have not scrupled to calumniate and libel him. When the Columbian Exposition was held in Chicago in 1892, and *"Christianity was still strong in North America, the name of Columbus was held in benediction"*. Since then, there have been renewed charges of Columbus being guilty of racism, barbaric and cruel treatment of Indians, and introducing African slavery into the new world. It may be added here that such charges have been stimulated by the continued power of the "Black Legend" *(la leyenda negra)*, i.e., politically-motivated historical writing by enemies of Spain who were intent on demonizing Spain and its colonization of the Americas. For Fr. Hardon, it is clear that *"the real ground for [continued] animosity against Columbus is the fact that he brought the Catholic Faith to the New World."*

Our distinguished author has written an inspiring work that pays due tribute to Columbus as a missionary Apostle who with the aid of a Spain that was faithful to the Church and the Roman Pontiffs helped spread the Gospel to millions. There is an important message to be drawn from his life. *"America discovered by him had to be evangelized. America today has to be re-evangelized"*. Serious obstacles to this re-evangelization (including an *"insurgent paganism"*) are identified and examined. Fr. Hardon's judgment on Columbus' life is poignant: *"Not unlike his Master, who was crucified and died abandoned by His own disciples, Columbus entered eternity without anyone paying any attention. He died estranged from his own contemporaries. In fact, he died in disgrace. That too is a deep lesson. The price of bringing souls to Christ is suffering."*

Fr. Hardon has written yet another book to inspire readers with a love of the Catholic Faith.

James Likoudis
President Emeritus, Catholics United for the Faith (CUF)

TABLE OF CONTENTS

FOREWORD		iii
I	**THE CATHOLIC DISCOVERY OF AMERICA**	1
	Why Speak About the Catholic Discovery of America	2
	Isabella the Catholic	5
	Christopher Columbus the Catholic	6
II	**CHRISTOPHER COLUMBUS THE CATHOLIC**	13
	Zealous Faith in Christ's Divinity	13
	Book of Prophecies	15
	Franciscan Tertiary	19
	Defense of Columbus' Character	21
III	**IN DEFENSE OF CHRISTOPHER COLUMBUS THE CATHOLIC**	25
	His Critics	25
	Defenders of the Native Indians	27
	African Slavery	28
	Appraisal of Christopher Columbus	29
IV	**THE BLESSED VIRGIN MARY AND THE CATHOLIC DISCOVERY OF AMERICA**	31
	Before Guadalupe	32
	Our Lady Appears to Juan Diego	33
	The Shrine of Our Lady of Guadalupe	36
	The Miraculous Conversion of Millions	37
V	**THE POPES AND THE CATHOLIC DISCOVERY OF AMERICA**	41
	Papal Loyalty in Pre-Columbian Spain	41
	The Papacy Abandoned and Discovered	43
	Pontifical America	44
	Epilogue	47
	Closing Prayer	47
VI	**FIVE HUNDRED YEARS SINCE COLUMBUS: LESSONS OF THE CHURCH'S HISTORY**	49
	Missionary Zeal	50
	The Witness of Martyrdom	52
	Conformism	55
	Marital Stability and Morality	57
	Our Responsibility	58

I
CHRISTOPHER COLUMBUS AND THE CATHOLIC DISCOVERY OF AMERICA

We are addressing ourselves to the subject of *The Catholic Discovery of America*. This year (1992) is the five hundredth anniversary of the discovery of America by Christopher Columbus. It is also the five hundredth anniversary of the birth of Christianity in the Western world. It is, finally, the five hundredth anniversary of the beginnings of the Catholic Church in North and South America.

Our Holy Father, Pope John Paul II, is coming to Central America on October 12th of this year to the Island of San Salvador where Columbus first landed in the New World. The Pope's pilgrimage will be in gratitude to God for planting the true faith in America. It will also be an earnest prayer to God for a strengthening of this faith where it has weakened and for a restoration of this faith where, as it has in millions, been lost.

Much has happened in the five hundred years since the Catholic faith was brought to America. There have been marvels of grace performed by the Catholic Church in the Western Hemisphere during the past half millennium. But much, very much, has still to be done.

Our purpose in these lectures is to develop our basic theme, which I call *The Catholic Discovery of America*. Our focus will not be on the discovery of America, which is obvious. It will be on the *Catholic* discovery of America which, I assure you, is not obvious.

What do we mean by the Catholic discovery of America?

- We mean the discovery of America by Spain, a country that for 700 years had suffered martyrdom under Islam, in defense of the Catholic Faith.

- We mean the discovery of America made possible by the apostolic zeal of Isabella I, the Catholic Queen of Spain.

After seven centuries, the Moors were finally driven out of Spain in the year 1491; 1492 came on the heels of seven centuries of martyrdom.

- We mean the discovery of America achieved by the Catholic genius of Christopher Columbus.

- We mean the discovery that was inspired by the Catholic vision of the Franciscans in Spain, without whom Columbus could never have been able to undertake his voyage to what became the new world.

- We mean the discovery of America that planted the seed of the Catholic Faith through the missionaries who evangelized the Americas and, how happy I am to say, and covered with the blood of many martyrs including my own Jesuit confreres.

- We mean the discovery that was blessed by Our Lady of Guadalupe during the lifetime of Fernando Columbus, the youngest son and biographer of his father, Christopher Columbus.

- We mean the discovery that was seen by the Roman Pontiffs as the dawn of a new era in Catholic evangelization.

- We mean the discovery that should inspire us to preserve, to purify and to promote the faith that so many of our forbearers since 1492 have labored, suffered and died for, so that we might be believing Catholics today.

In the lectures planned for our series, we shall look in sequence at each of these meanings of the Catholic discovery of America. My hope is that these lectures will not be lectures in any ordinary academic sense, but lessons of faith as we mark a turning point in American Catholic history.

Why Speak About the Catholic Discovery of America?

Before we begin to look at the Catholic faith of Isabella and Columbus, the two people most responsible for the discovery of the new world, there is more than passing value in asking ourselves a very basic and ordinary question: Why should we even consider the *Catholic* discovery of America?

There are many reasons, and they are all powerful motives for defending what crucially needs to be defended. That except for the Catholic Church, there would not have been a discovery of the New World as we know it. There would not have been the providential opening of two continents to the true Faith. There would not have been the perfect timing between the loss of six whole nations in Europe who were lost to Catholic unity and the rise of new countries where, by now, hundreds of millions have lived with faith in Christ's Real Presence in the Holy Eucharist and died as faithful sons and daughters of the Roman Catholic Church.

God timed - He timed - the breakdown of Catholic unity in so much of continental Europe. England, Wales, Scotland, Norway, Sweden and Denmark were completely torn away from union with the Bishop of Rome, and much of Germany and much of Switzerland along with them. If ever St. Paul's words were verified that *where sin abounds, there grace even more abounds*, it is unspeakably true in the perfect timing by God between the loss of the Faith in so much of continental Europe and the discovery of a new world that, by now, in the last 500 years, hundreds of millions of Catholics have lived and died in the Western Hemisphere.

We know (how well we know by now) what an *authentic* Catholic is:

- An authentic Catholic believes unqualifyingly that the Child in Mary's arms on Christmas morning was her God.

- A Catholic believes that when Christ left the Earth in visible form on Ascension Thursday, He did not leave the Earth into which He was born. Why not? Because we believe in the Real Presence of Jesus on Earth in the Holy Eucharist.

- An authentic Catholic believes that one man, the Bishop of Rome, is Christ's Vicar and final court of appeal on *what we must believe* and *how we must behave*.

I repeat, for the last 500 years, hundreds of millions of people have lived and died believing what we've just identified as *authentic* Catholic Christianity, but only because there has been a Catholic discovery of America. As you read the books and periodicals anticipating, now during the present year, commemorating the quincentennial Columbian anniversary, we are struck by these books and periodicals to be almost totally secular in their interpretation of what really took place in 1492. Geography, Astronomy and History, Economics and Politics, Sociology and Paleontology are woven into a huge literary tapestry in which God and religion and Jesus Christ are scarcely mentioned and from which every named Catholic is scrupulously excluded.

In pondering lectures over the last several months, I thought I would begin by describing what happened in 1891 when, as I'm sure you know, there was the four hundredth anniversary of the discovery of America.

And do you know why it would have been relevant to talk about it in Chicago? Because, Chicago was where this international Columbian anniversary took place. You read what people said about Columbus and about the discovery of America from the proceedings of the Columbian exposition in 1892 - you read it and you weep. Whatever else we'd better know, we better know what really happened in 1492.

Some writers openly accuse Columbus of invading the land of the American Indians. Others charge Columbus with introducing slavery. Still others claim that if anyone is to be given credit for discovering America, it should be Eric the Scandinavian, centuries before Columbus.

We who believe in Divine Providence know that the discovery of America was not coincidental. I don't hesitate saying it was planned by God from all eternity. Just before His Ascension into Heaven, Our Lord told His disciples, I quote, "You will be my witnesses not only in Jerusalem but throughout Judea and Samaria and indeed to the ends of the earth" (Acts 1:8).

Our task here will be to see how the prophecy of Christ was fulfilled just five centuries ago, when the followers of Christ became His witnesses, and as I've told so many of you, our Lord's words in the Acts of the Apostles from which I've quoted, when He said you will be my witnesses, the Greek of the inspired text is: "You will be my martyrs" literally, "to the ends of the earth" including the Western Hemisphere and, dare I say, including Chicago. My plan for the rest of this lecture is to talk about two people: Isabella, the Catholic and Christopher Columbus, the Discoverer.

Isabella the Catholic

We cannot begin to understand the Catholic discovery of America without knowing something of Isabella I, Queen of Castile. Born in 1451, she died in 1506. In 1469 she married Ferdinand V, King of Aragon, and then, together with him, united the two countries into the modern nation of Spain. Among their five children was Catherine of Aragon who married Henry VIII; the woman whom Henry VIII discarded. Yet it was Catherine of Aragon's parents who were responsible under God for promoting and making possible the discovery of the New World.

Isabella was a deeply religious woman. Her strong character joined with an ardent faith has made her the object of violent criticism for her role in the Spanish Inquisition. The Inquisition was not a mistake, but whatever mistakes Isabella made (and she made mistakes) no one could possibly question her strong, heroic devotion to Catholic truth. Among the many letters that Isabella received from the popes is one from Pope Sixtus IV who wrote to her, and I quote, "Very dear daughter, we know that your person is distinguished by many royal virtues through the divine munificence; but we have commended none more than your devotion to God and your enduring love for the orthodox faith" (Walsh, Isabella of Spain, 264). God made sure that when America was to be discovered, two people of heroic stature in their devotion to the Catholic faith, Isabella and Columbus, should have been responsible for the world-changing phenomenon.

By 1492, Columbus had made three unsuccessful efforts to persuade the Iberian royalty to authorize his search for the Indies by crossing the Atlantic. Twice in Spain and once in Portugal, royal commissions decided against financing the expedition of Columbus. A third effort to get Spanish support failed in early January 1492.

It was then that Queen Isabella entered American history. Her cause for canonization was introduced but violently, militantly opposed by those who then, not wanting a resurgent Catholicism in the New World, I will say, postponed the canonization of Queen Isabella. Her husband, Ferdinand, did not think that Columbus had good judgment in hoping to reach the Far East by going to the west. Ferdinand did not take Columbus seriously. Here is the way Ferdinand was thinking: "Here is a foreigner, (Columbus was Italian by birth) already turned down by the Portuguese for his dreamy scheme. Add to this Columbus' reserved, some would call it a secretive, character." "No," said Ferdinand. "Columbus should not be allowed to damage the reputation of Spain by venturing on a fanciful voyage that would only send a hundred or so men to their watery graves."

Queen Isabella did not agree with her husband. She prayed and she fasted that she might be able to persuade her husband to agree with her in backing Christopher Columbus. She had too much experience with God's mysterious ways to reduce Columbus to a starry seaman who did not know what he was talking about. Columbus later described the skepticism of everyone else (except Queen Isabella) about crossing the Atlantic to reach the Indies. "In all men" Columbus wrote, "there was disbelief. But to the Queen, My Lady, God gave the spirit of understanding and great courage and made her heiress of all as a dear and much-loved daughter." (Walsh, 337)

The rugged holiness of Isabella is revealed in every biographer of the Queen. It was in large measure due to her zeal for the preservation of the Catholic faith that she, like Joan of Arc, led on horseback the Spanish troops to recover her country from the seven centuries of control by the Moors of Islam. It was because she saw the harm being done to the Catholic Church by the pseudo-converts, called *conversos*, that she organized, with the full approval of the Holy Father, the now much-maligned Spanish Inquisition.

It was this same woman who prayed much, who had a great devotion to the Blessed Sacrament, who had a regular confessor; and she went to the Sacrament of Confession frequently. In her humility (and this is part of her writing) she recalls how she was reprimanded more than once by her confessor for her vanity in dress. It was this saintly woman who saw, with God's grace, in Christopher Columbus the man destined by God to open a new world to the Gospel of Jesus Christ.

Christopher Columbus the Catholic

In the past 500 years, several thousand books have been written about Columbus. Depending on the author, myriad aspects of his character are described and analyzed. I've read many books in anticipation of this series. It all depends on whom you read, but most of the biographers of Columbus tend to explain why it was Columbus who discovered America. They ask and they don't have the answer. Why, for example, the Native Americans did not discover Europe. Many people long before Columbus had a sophisticated knowledge of astronomy, which is the basis of what we call celestial navigation. Why have the Chinese or the Arabs not ventured across the Atlantic Ocean? In the Middle Ages, China was the wealthiest nation in the world. They had tremendous power over the seas. So, too, the Moslems had extended Islam from the Mideast to the farthest reaches of Western Europe and the most distant lands of the Far East. Why not the Chinese? Why not the Moslems? Why Columbus?

Anyone who knows the history of Chinese and Moslem societies in the 15th Century would have said that they, and not Europeans, would be the persons to cross the Pacific or Atlantic Oceans. To us it seems incredible that for centuries, many centuries, most of what we identify with the ancient world did not even know that what we now call the *New World* existed.

There is no natural explanation of why it should have been Columbus, but once we draw on the resources of Revelation we can see why. It was because the God who became man wanted His message of salvation to be extended by strong Catholic believers to people who were still walking in darkness and had been untouched by the Gospel.

From this perspective, the deep, even aggressive Catholic Faith of Isabella and Columbus provides the explanation. They were deep believers. They were also aggressive missionaries. Needless to say, in our day 500 years later, we too might, then, need a deep faith, and I mean it, an aggressive, apostolic zeal.

In our next lecture, we plan to see in more detail how Columbus put his faith into practice. Our present focus is on the manifestations of his faith as seen in the detailed, day by day log which Columbus kept from August 3, 1492 when he left Spain to October 12, 1492 when he set foot in the New World. I have a number of logs of Columbus at my disposal, but to make sure I'd have the latest available in print, I ordered a brand new copy. To make sure I'd get it in time, I asked them to send it to me express mail. You read that log of Christopher Columbus and you are overwhelmed by the man's deep Catholic faith. The log begins with a prayer: "In the Name of our Lord Jesus Christ." The spirit of this opening prayer pervades the entire log. Throughout the log Columbus is constantly invoking the Name of Christ or God or Divine Providence. He is thanking our Lord and expressing his confidence in the power of the Almighty to bring to realization what for so many years people were telling him was a wild mirage. I would like to now quote and give you the dates from Columbus' log revealing the simplicity and the depth of his faith.

August 12th, Sunday:

"Today, praised be to God, I arrived at Gomora and sent a boat ashore."

August 19th, Sunday:

"My enterprise is in God's hands."

August 24th, Friday:

"By divine providence the wind shifted and we made some progress."

August 25th, Saturday:

"God must have planned it that way."

August 30th, Thursday:

"The rudder is almost finished, praise God."

September 17th, Monday:

"All the indications of land come from the west, where I trust Almighty God in whose hands are all victories, will soon deliver us to land."

September 19th, Wednesday:

"It is my desire to go directly to the Indies and not get sidetracked with islands that I shall see on the return passage, God willing."

September 23rd, Sunday:

"When the sea made up considerably without wind, they [my crew] were astonished. I saw this as a sign from God, and it was very helpful to me. Such a sign has not appeared since Moses led the Jews out of Egypt, and they dared not lay a violent hand on him because of the miracle that God had wrought. As with Moses when he led his people out of captivity, my people were humbled by this act of the Almighty."

September 24th, Monday:

"I am having serious trouble with my crew, despite the signs of land that we have and those given to us by Almighty God. In fact, the more God shows the men manifest signs that we are near land, the more their impatience and inconstancy increases, and the more indignant they become against me."

September 25th, Tuesday:

"At sunset, Martin [one of the crew] mounted the stern of the *Pinta* and with great joy called to me that he saw land and claimed the reward [to the one who first sights land]. When I heard this stated so positively, I fell to my knees to give thanks to our Lord, and Martin said *Gloria in excelsis Deo* with his people. My people did the same thing."

October 5th, Friday:

"The wind abated somewhat during the night. The sea is pleasant and calm. Many thanks be given to God."

October 7th, Sunday:

"Joy turned to dismay as the day progressed, for by evening we had found no land and had to face the reality that it was only an illusion. God did offer us, however, a small token of comfort: many large flocks of birds flew over, coming from the North and flying to the Southwest. They were more varied in kind than any we had seen before, and they were land birds."

October 9th, Tuesday:

"All night long we heard birds passing. We must be very close to landfall, thanks be to God."

October 11th, Thursday:

"As is our custom, Vespers were said in the late afternoon, and a special thanksgiving was offered to God for giving us renewed hope through the many signs of land He has provided. I now believe that the light I saw earlier was a sign from God and that it was truly the first positive indication of land."

October 12th, Friday:

"At dawn we saw naked people, and I went ashore in the ship's boat …I unfurled the royal banner and the captains brought the flags which displayed a large green cross with the letters "F" [Ferdinand] and "Y" [Isabella] at the left and right side of the cross. …To this land I gave the name San Salvador, in honor of our Blessed Lord."

Throughout the log, Columbus makes it clear why he and his men are sailing across the Atlantic. It was to spread the Good News of Salvation and convert the natives to Christianity.

In his opening introduction of the log, he addresses the King and Queen of Spain. "Your Highnesses decided to send me, Christopher Columbus, to the regions of India to see the princes there and the peoples and the lands, and to learn of their disposition and of everything, and the measures which could be taken for their conversion to our Holy Catholic Faith."

Columbus went on to identify the chief prince of the Indies, who is called the great Khan, which Columbus said means the *King of Kings*. And then in a two-sentence statement he tells us why we not only may, but we must call Columbus' coming to the western world the Catholic Discovery of America.

> "I informed Your Highnesses the Great Khan and its predecessors had sent to Rome many times to beg for men learned in our Holy Faith, so that his people might be instructed therein, and that the Holy Father had never furnished them, and therefore, many peoples believing in idolatries and receiving among themselves sects of perdition - were lost.
>
> Your Highnesses, as Catholic Christians and Princes devoted to the Holy Christian faith and to the spreading of this faith and as enemies of the Muslim sect and of all idolatries and heresies, ordered that I should go east, but not by land as is customary. I was to go by way of the west, whence until today we do not

> know with certainty that anyone has ever gone there. He sent me that I might bring the true faith to the Indians."

This missionary theme is sustained throughout the published writings of Columbus. I think I should insert here, but it is not my manuscript, that how much we've been educated, how many years we've gone to school, most of us, if not all of us, have been taught a misinterpretation of history. As Catholics, however, we had better wake up! because the same forces that are now calling Christopher Columbus an invader or slave trader are those who are using every means at their disposal to crush the faith, that we would not have to do unless the missionary, Christopher Columbus, had discovered the New World.

It is of more than passing value to read what Columbus wrote on his arrival in the New World. It contradicts so many myths, not only about Columbus, but about his alleged cruelty towards the native Indians whom he found in America. He is still writing on October 12, 1492...

> "The people here ...are friendly and well-dispositioned... who bear no arms except for small spears and they have no iron. I want the natives to develop a friendly attitude towards us because I know they are a people who can be made free and converted to our Holy Catholic Faith, more by love than by force. I therefore gave red caps to some and glass beads to others. They hung the beads around their necks ... and they took great pleasure in this and became so friendly that it was a marvel. They traded and gave everything they had with good will, but it seems to me they have very little and are poor in everything. I warned my men to take nothing from the people without giving something in exchange."

This quotation from his log on October 12, 1492 may seem to be or have been a bit longer than other quotations that I gave in this lecture, but they are not by any means exhaustive. To show how thoroughly Catholic, how deeply zealous and how courageous Columbus was, the more you read of his own writings, the more they reveal what we in our day need to see: that the discovery of America was not accidental, but deeply providential. It was not by chance but eternally designed by God.

In the light of what we have so far seen, we not only *may* but we *must* see how the Catholic discovery of America was Catholic in many ways, but in none more evidently than the apostolic zeal of Queen Isabella and Christopher Columbus.

My hope, my deep hope is that the graces that God is giving during this quincentennial year will arouse in all of us something of the zeal to convert our fellow Americans to the true Faith. More than once we have excluded coincidence and chance from the events that led to the discovery of the new world. God had, and has, a profoundly wise plan. It is up to us to recognize His plan and cooperate with His grace for the extension of the Kingdom of Christ and its consolidation in our own land.

Christopher Columbus died in 1506. Not unlike his Master, who was crucified and died abandoned by His own disciples, Columbus entered eternity without anyone paying any attention. He died estranged from his own contemporaries. In fact, he died in disgrace. That too is a deep lesson. The price of bringing souls to Christ is suffering.

As one historian of Columbus regretfully writes, *"It is a very strange commentary on man's forgetfulness of his fellow-man that Christopher Columbus, who had filled so large a place in the world at the close of the fifteenth century, should die and be buried without any unusual expression of public sorrow or even mention by historian or chronologer."* (Robert Fuson, The Log of Christopher Columbus, p. 237)

Columbus seems to have died a failure, but God always provides. The same year, 1506, that Christopher Columbus died, St. Francis Xavier was born. Talk about divine timing. Xavier, as you know, is the Church's universal patron (I should add, along with the Little Flower) of the missions. Christopher Columbus gave us a mission. He brought the true faith to our land. After five centuries, thank God there are many strongly believing Catholics in the western world. They were under no illusion. Many have discarded the Faith which they once professed. Many others are Catholics only in name. The deepest need of America is for that spiritual food which is Christ's revealed Truth brought to America 500 years ago. Please God we will put it into practice and realize the hopes of the Vicar of Christ, of Queen Isabella and of Christopher Columbus in our day.

II

CHRISTOPHER COLUMBUS THE CATHOLIC

Hundreds of biographies of Christopher Columbus have been written in the last five centuries. They range from the poetic to the highly critical. As a result, it is not always easy to identify the real Columbus from the person who is responsible for discovering the New World.

Our purpose here is not to sift through this library of Columbus biographies. It is simply to show that Columbus was not only a good man. He was extraordinary. He was the instrument of extraordinary grace. This, then, is our focus in this chapter. It is to see how God used a very human, human being, whose faith enabled him to achieve what most writers on Columbus do not recognize. It is one thing to say that Columbus discovered America. It is something else to realize that he opened the door to the most phenomenal spread of Christianity since the time of St. Paul.

There are those who say that Christopher Columbus died a saint. Certainly the sufferings he experienczed, especially from those to whom he was most devoted, chastened his heart and brought him close to God before he entered eternity. One thing we can say: his phenomenal career on earth was a heroic response to a sublime vocation. He was the destined herald of the true faith to half of the human race.

Our plan for understanding "Christopher Columbus, the Catholic" is to follow a chronological sequence. Given our necessary limitations, we shall highlight those aspects of his life that reveal what may be called the "mystic" behind the trained explorer.

Zealous Faith in Christ's Divinity

The exact date of Columbus' birth is unknown. Fourteen-thirty-six is one of the probable dates. What is more important is the fact of his baptism in the Dominican Church of St. Stephen in Genoa. All we know of his early life indicates that he was deeply pious. It is recorded of him that he assisted at daily Mass at a convent chapel where he first met his wife, Doña Philippa. What is more important however, than anything else, is that Columbus came into the world at the end of more than seven centuries of Moslem domination of the Spanish people. As we have already seen, he crossed the Atlantic and found the New World within one year of the Catholic re-conquest of the Iberian Peninsula.

English speaking people have only a vague idea of the struggle of the Spanish people to recover the Catholic freedom from Moslem oppression. Not coincidentally, in this quincentennial year of the discovery of America, the Catholic Bishops of Sudan issued a pastoral letter that could almost be called a commentary on the Islamic-liberated Spain from which Columbus sailed in 1492. The Sudanese hierarchy protest against the militant persecution of Catholics in their country. Islamic studies are mandatory for all students advancing to higher education. There is active discrimination against Catholics. Moslem propaganda against the Catholic Church is woven into all academic programs. The avowed purpose is to eradicate Christianity from the country. In fact, no less then twenty-four African nations have bound themselves behind the Koran to de-Christianize the whole continent.

As we read these facts, we are not surprised that the same country, in the same century, should have produced two men whose lives were shaped by centuries of defense of the Catholic faith against Moslem oppression of Christianity. St. Ignatius Loyola was a born Spaniard. Christopher Columbus was a Spaniard by adoption. Both men had the vision of extending the kingdom of Christ by a spiritual militancy that seems strange to a modern unbelieving mind. The key to understanding the faith of Christopher Columbus is the Moslem denial of Christ's divinity as the cardinal mystery of Christianity.

Woven into the Koran as a theological theme, and has since become the cornerstone of Islam, is the dogma that God could not have had a son and therefore that Jesus could not be one with Allah. "Jesus in Allah's eyes is in the same position as Adam," wrote Mohammed. "He created him of dust and then said to him, 'Be,' and he is." This was revealed by Gabriel and "whosoever disputes with you concerning Him (Jesus), we will summon our sons and your sons and our women and your women and we will humbly and solemnly invoke the curse of Allah upon those who lie." In one eloquent passage, Mohammed consigns all Trinitarian Christians to eternal doom.

They surely disbelieve who say, "Behold, Allah is the Messiah, Son of Mary." The Messiah himself said, "Children of Israel, worship Allah, my

Lord and your God." Whoever ascribes partners unto Allah, for him Allah has forbidden paradise. This abode is the fire. For evildoers there will be no relief. They surely disbelieve who say, "Behold Allah is the third of three," when there is no god save the one God. If they desist not from so saying, a painful doom will fall on those who disbelieve. The Messiah, Son of Mary, was no other than a messenger. Many were the messengers that passed away before him. See how God makes His signs clear to them (Christians); yet see how they are deluded away from the truth.

No Moslem who professes to accept the Koran questions these judgments about Jesus and His followers. Christ is for him only a great teacher and the precursor of Mohammed.

If there is one thing that stands out in the extensive writings of Christopher Columbus it is the divinity of Christ. Phrases like "our Lord Jesus Christ," and Christ "the Lord," recur in a way that leaves no doubt who Jesus Christ was in the faith of Christopher Columbus. He speaks of "Christ, who is the Son of God by nature." He quotes from St. Paul of "Christ Jesus before the beginning of time" (2 Timothy 1:9-10). He sees himself as contributing to the extension of Christ's kingdom when, "All the kings of the earth will bow down before Him, and all peoples will serve Him" (Psalm 72:11).

It is no wonder then that Columbus wants to share his faith with others. He believed that there is nothing more important than to proclaim faith in Christ to all the nations. Jesus Christ, Columbus declared, is the One "Whom we recognize as the true God Who was to be worshiped, not only among the people of Israel, but among all peoples, in such a way that all their false gods must be cast from their temples and from the hearts of their worshippers" (Christopher Columbus, *Book of Prophecies*, Folio 22).

Against this background, there is only one logical conclusion. The underlying motive of Columbus' historic voyage was the conversion of those who did not know Christ as the living Son of God Who became the Son of Mary. His favorite prayer, said in Latin, was *"Jesu cum Maria sit nobis in via"*, which means "May Jesus with Mary be with us on the way." For Columbus this *way* meant both the voyage through time into eternity and the voyage in time to bring Mary's faith in her divine Son to a still unbelieving world.

Book of Prophecies

One of the least known facts about Christopher Columbus is his *Book of Prophecies (Libro de las profecias)*. Even among biographers who refer to this writing, they mention it only in passing or use it as evidence of Columbus' visionary personality. As we have already seen, Columbus was no visionary. He was gifted not only with a deep faith but with what may be called a mystical understanding of God's will for the world. The *Book of Prophecies* is one of our primary sources for understanding Columbus. In spite of the title, the *Book of Prophecies* is not a series of predictions made by Christopher Columbus. It is rather a collection of prophetic passages from Sacred Scripture which Columbus related to his Great Enterprise of the Indies. Written in 1502, after his third voyage to the New World, this work provides us with a clear picture of how Columbus saw himself. He saw himself as a servant of the Lord who, though unworthy, was chosen by God to discover what we now know is the Western Hemisphere. The original manuscript of the *Book of Prophecies* is written in two languages: the Castilian Spanish that reflects Portuguese influence and Latin which Columbus quotes at length from the Fathers of the Church and the Vulgate text of the Bible. We get some idea of the spirit of this book from the letter which Columbus wrote to King Ferdinand and Queen Isabella. He says:

At this time I have seen and put in study to look into all the Scriptures ...which our Lord opened to my understanding – I could sense His hand upon me – so that it became clear to me that it was feasible to navigate from here to the Indies, and He gave me the will to execute the idea ...I have already said that for the execution of the enterprise of the Indies, neither reason nor mathematics nor world maps were profitable to me: rather the prophecy of Isaiah was completely fulfilled. And this is what I wish to report here for the consideration of Your Highnesses (Book of Prophecies, Folos 4, 4 rvs., 5 rvs).

Most of the prophecies from Isaiah which Columbus quotes refer to the restoration of Jerusalem and its future glory. Once again Islam comes into the picture. Constantinople, the gateway to the Far East fell into Moslem hands. By the year 1500, the Turks had conquered all the territory up to the very edge of the republic of Venice. It was not until the battle of Lepanto (October 7, 1571) that Christian forces stemmed the Moslem tide into Europe. Ever since, October 7th is the feast of Our Lady of the Rosary, to whom the Pope credited the saving of Christendom.

What is not commonly known is that the growing power of the followers of Mohammed had closed the normal pathway from Europe to the Orient. In God's providence, this is what occasioned the search for another way to the Indies. Most historians claim that this was the dominant motive for Columbus going west so that the wealth of the East might be found. The *Book of Prophecies* shows the opposite. Commercial interests were certainly prominent in the minds of others. But Columbus had deeper spiritual interests at heart. It was surely part of God's mysterious design that Columbus should have planted the true faith in the New World at the same time that Islam was overrunning Africa, the Near East, and was being driven out of Southern Europe.

As one reads the *Book of Prophecies*, the spirit of the Crusades stands out. For centuries the Crusaders, under Papal inspiration, sought to liberate the holy City of Jerusalem from Moslem domination. This is the underlying theme of the *Book of Prophecies*, but with one remarkable difference. Columbus sought not so much the physical deliverance of the Holy Land. His aim was to extend the Faith which makes the Holy Land holy. As he told the Spanish sovereigns, "If there is faith, you are bound to have victory from the enterprise" *(Ibidem)*. As a matter of fact, Columbus' son Diego achieved exactly what his father had told him to do in his last will and testament. *"When your days are over,"* the prophet told King David, *"and you go to be with your fathers, I will raise up your offspring to succeed you, one of your own sons ...he will be the one who will build a house for me"* quoted by Columbus from I Chronicles, 17: 11,12 (Book of Prophecies folio 56). Diego Columbus fulfilled his father's wish when he built the first Catholic Church in America (Hispaniola).

Columbus had no doubt that he was the servant of the Lord, but in a very definite sense. He was the man who saw himself chosen by God "to fulfill my purpose," as Isaiah had prophesied (Isaiah 46:11). It was to be a "holy enterprise." This vocation came from the Holy Spirit. It was nothing less than to liberate the nations that walk in darkness and bring them to the light of Christ. Columbus quotes from the Prophet Jeremiah who saw himself as chosen by God: "I formed you in the womb. I knew you before you were born. I set you apart. I set you as a prophet to the nations" (Jeremiah 1:5). After giving this quotation, Columbus speaks to the Lord, "This is what You ordained beforehand according to Your good pleasure, such [prophesies] as were written in Your book about me, in conformity with your secret purpose" (*Book of Prophecies*, Folio 15).

Many people, on reading this would accuse Columbus of either a psychotic delusion or of consummate pride. But this would be contrary to fact. Before God, Columbus saw himself as totally subject to the will of God. This after all, is the essence of humility.

What especially stands out in the *Book of Prophecies* is the principal source of Columbus' motivation to convert the people of the Indies to "our Holy Faith." It was his faith in the word of God revealed in the Scriptures which inspired him to do what was thought humanly impossible. Writing to Ferdinand and Isabella, Columbus shared with them his trust in God as revealed in the Bible.

The working out of all things was entrusted by our Lord to each person, (but it happens) *in conformity with His sovereign will, even though He gives advice to many …I found our Lord well-disposed toward my heart's desire, and he gave me the spirit of intelligence for the task…Who doubts that this illumination was from the Holy Spirit? He* [the Spirit], *with marvelous rays of light, consoled me through the holy and sacred Scriptures, a strong and clear testimony ,…encouraging me to proceed and continually without ceasing for a moment, they inflame me with a sense of great urgency.* (Book of Prophecies, Fols. 5 rvs., 4)

As early as 1493, Columbus wrote a letter to the Royal Treasurer of Spain in which he speaks of the discovery of the New World as a great victory. Yet, it was not a victory by force of arms but a victory of bringing the truth to people who were sitting in the darkness of unbelief. He wrote,

Since our Redeemer gave this victory to our most illustrious King and Queen and to their famous realms, in so great a manner, it is fitting for all Christendom to rejoice and to make celebrations and give solemn thanks to the Holy Trinity with many solemn prayers for the great exultation which it will have and the turning of so many peoples to our holy Faith.

As an afterthought, Columbus assured the Royal Treasurer that there would also be temporal benefits not only to Spain but to all Christians. What must be emphasized, however, is that this was an afterthought. The primary reason for thanking God is because so many people would come to know Jesus Christ and become members of the One, True Church.

We get some idea of how literally Columbus saw his discovery as a fulfillment of divine predilection. On Sunday, October 14th, two days after he landed at San Salvador, he is describing the people who stood on the shore as they watched Columbus and his crew bring their ships to land.

By the signs they made, I think they were asking if we came from heaven. One old man even climbed into the boat we were towing, and others shouted in loud voices to everyone on the beach, saying, "Come see the men from heaven, bring them food and drink." Many men and women came, each one with something. They threw themselves on the sand and raised their hands to the sky, shouting for us to come ashore, while giving thanks to God. I kept going this morning despite the pleas of the people to come ashore, for I was alarmed at seeing that the entire island is surrounded by a large reef. Between the reef and the island it remained deep, and this port is large enough to hold all the ships of Christendom.

The next day Columbus reached another island where he hauled in the sails. He adds the statement, "To this island I gave the name Sancta Maria de la Concepcion." He had no doubt that his *Book of Prophecies* was being fulfilled to the last detail.

Franciscan Tertiary

To understand the character of Christopher Columbus we must say something of his association with St. Francis of Assisi. Almost as soon as St. Francis formed the Franciscan Friars, he established the Third Order Secular of his new community. The substance of the original Rule of these tertiaries is contained in St. Francis' *Letter to All the Faithful*. To read this letter is to see the life and spirit of Christopher Columbus. St. Francis' directives read like a catalogue of what Columbus sincerely tried to put into practice.

- We should confess all our sins to a priest and receive from him the Body and Blood of our Lord Jesus Christ.

- We must bring forth fruits befitting repentance and love our neighbors as ourselves. Anyone who will not or can not love his neighbor as himself should at least do him good and not do him any harm.

- Those who have been entrusted with the power of judging others should pass judgment mercifully, just as they themselves hope to obtain mercy.

- We are also bound to fast and avoid vice and sin, taking care not to give way to excess in food and drink, and we must be Catholics.

- It is not for us to be wise and calculating in the world's fashion; we should be guileless, lowly and pure.

All that we know about Columbus testifies to his having lived up to his Franciscan Rule. We know that he would wear the Franciscan habit, especially when he appeared before the Royalty or nobility. Except for the Franciscans with whom he stayed before leaving on his historic voyage, he would never have received the entree to Ferdinand and Isabella which opened the door to the New World. He went to confession to Franciscan priests. He would spend long periods of time in worshiping before the Blessed Sacrament in Franciscan chapels. When he left Palos, Spain on August 3, 1492 to cross the Atlantic, he left his son in the care of the Franciscans at their monastery.

There was one feature of Columbus' Franciscan spirituality that by now we have seen was dominant in his historic discovery. It is the zeal of St. Francis, as expressed in his Rule of Life, "To go among the Saracens or other unbelievers." As we know, Francis himself did the incredible thing of personally visiting the Moslem Sultan in the Near East to bring him the Gospel of the Christian faith. To this day, Franciscans are the authorized guardians of the sacred places in the Holy Land.

Throughout the eight centuries of Christian history before Columbus, we find the three features that typify the life and work of the discoverer of the New World:

1. A militant Islam which was bent on converting Christian idolaters who worshiped Isa (Jesus) not only as the *Ibn Maryam* (Son of Mary) but as *Ibn Allah* (Son of God). This militancy is part of the Islamic faith.

2. A defensive Christianity which saw itself under the growing power of a people whose religion was to remove idolatry from the face of the earth.

3. An organized strategy among Christian believers to defend themselves, even by the sword, but in the spirit of their Founder to propagate the gospel among unbelievers who did not believe that God became man to die for us on the cross and to remain with us in His physical humanity in the Holy Eucharist.

We have seen something of the first two aspects of what may be called the Franciscanism of Christopher Columbus. What needs to be stressed, however, is Columbus' faith in the Real Presence of Christ in the Blessed

Sacrament. St. Francis could not have been more bluntly clear than what he wrote in his Admonitions which were basic directives for his followers, whether religious or the faithful in the world.

God the Son is equal to the Father and so He too can be seen only in the same way as the Father and the Holy Spirit. That is why all those were condemned who saw our Lord Jesus Christ in His humanity but did not see or believe in spirit in His divinity, that He was the true Son of God. In the same way now, all those are damned who see the Sacrament of the Body of Christ which is consecrated on the altar in the form of bread and wine by the words of our Lord in the hands of the priest, and do not see or believe in spirit and in God that This is really the most holy Body and Blood of our Lord Jesus Christ.

These words of the gentle St. Francis are a commentary on the faith of Christopher Columbus. Like Francis, Columbus believed that Jesus Christ was on earth in His living Humanity. Not unlike Francis, Columbus was rigidly adamant in extending this Faith to the farthest reaches of the globe.

Defense of Columbus' Character

The biographers of Columbus, as we have seen, range from ardent admirers to virulent enemies. The hostility of his critics has taken many forms. But one group of detractors should be answered in any appraisal of Christopher Columbus the Catholic. They are those who claim that Columbus lived with another woman than his wife. In our day, this calumny is accepted even by otherwise believing Catholics. They go so far as to say that this was the main reason why Columbus was never canonized. All serious historians of Columbus now recognize that this detraction goes back only to the late seventeenth Century.

What are the facts? Within two years of his marriage to Phillipa, she died shortly after giving birth to Columbus' first son, Diego. At the time of his wife's death, Columbus was thirty years old. It caused Columbus deep grief, so much so that his early biographers say that the death of Phillipa occurred at the same time when his hair turned suddenly gray.

Some ten years later, in the autumn of 1487, Columbus married his second wife, Doña Beatrix Enriquez. She was a member of one of the oldest aristocratic families in Spain. Fernando Columbus, the only child of this union, was born in August of the next year.

What gave rise to the calumny? It was an obscure note made by one Nicolao Antonion, librarian in Spain. He came across a copy of Columbus' last will in which a pension was provided for Beatrix Enriquez, "mother of his second son, Fernando." Columbus noted in his will that he is making this provision "for the relief of my conscience." Antonio reads into these words of Columbus what almost two centuries of history simply deny, namely that Beatrix was not Columbus' wife but only his concubine.

After Antonio, the illegitimacy of Fernando Columbus became the target of all his father's hostile biographers. This has occasioned what may be considered the single most researched defense of a historic character. Only the main lines of this defense can be given here.

Columbus was a man of deep religious faith which absolutely excluded illicit love. In Columbus' own language this sin would consign his soul to eternal punishment. His frequent reception of the Sacrament of Confession testifies to his sensitivity of conscience.

Everything we know about the life of Columbus witnesses to his lifelong practice of continence and chastity. This was in marked contrast to the practice of his Spanish followers in Hispaniola.

Columbus was a man who knew the world and knew how to cope with its temptations. None of his contemporaries, even those who envied his achievements, ever accused him of giving in to impurity. Columbus' life was pure in an atmosphere of impurity.

The family of Arana to which Beatrix belonged, had the reputation for extraordinary piety. As with Columbus, her religion was a powerful protection against her fall.

During the voyages of Columbus, the members of both his first and second family were brought together in frequent social relationship. It is unthinkable that those who belonged to his first family would have permitted or submitted to contact with Columbus and Beatrix if the latter were living dishonestly.

From 1487 to 1494, Columbus left both his sons, Diego, the son of his first wife and Fernando, the son of Beatrix, in the custody of Beatrix. The very fame of Columbus after 1492 precluded the possibility of Beatrix not being Columbus' lawful wedded wife. Yet not a word of scandal is recorded among the contemporaries of Christopher Columbus.

Bartholomew Columbus brought his two nephews, Diego and Fernando, to Queen Isabella and presented them at court. Isabella immediately received them with respect and honor and appointed them as pages in her retinue. The Queen's delicate conscience and recognized sanctity ruled out the possibility that Fernando was illegitimate.

All the foregoing might have been unnecessary except that the English speaking world has been so critical of Christopher Columbus. We must distinguish, however, between English biographers who shared Columbus' Catholic faith and those, no matter how erudite, whose religious ancestry did not exclude what Catholic Christianity believes is a grave sin.

It is imperative for any objective study of the character of Christopher Columbus to sift the chaff from the wheat in defending the virtue of the discoverer of America.

III

IN DEFENSE OF CHRISTOPHER COLUMBUS THE CATHOLIC

There are few great men in history who do not have both their ardent admirers and their virulent traducers. Christopher Columbus is no exception. But there is one main difference in the case of Columbus. We can identify his critics by their religious affiliation or ideology.

The discoverer of America was a zealous, even militant, Roman Catholic. He lived in the very generation when six whole nations in Europe broke with the Catholic Church to create what we have come to know as Protestantism. The Spain from which Columbus sailed to discover the New World had just succeeded in delivering its people from seven hundred years of Moslem domination. In Islam, Christians are idolaters who dare to give divine honors to Jesus, the Son of Mary, because they believe that He is the Son of the living God. Finally, on the eve of Columbus' historic voyage, the Moriscoes (professed Moorish converts still Mohammedan at heart) were allowed to leave Spain to protect them from the animosity of the people. In the eyes of the Spaniards, the Moriscoes were pseudo-converts from Judaism who were a threat to the stability of the Spanish nation.

It is not surprising therefore, that Christopher Columbus' adversaries go back to the early sixteenth century. Added to those who opposed him on principle were those who were hostile because of his phenomenal achievement and consequent fame. No one envies a failure! Columbus' achievement ranks as one of the greatest in recorded human history. Envy dogged his steps from the moment he set foot on El Salvador, October 12, 1492.

His Critics

We can trace the first beginnings of hostility to Columbus after he had discovered the New Indies and the Spanish sovereigns established their authority over these lands. A certain Bobadilla was appointed by the Spanish Crown as Governor General over the Indies. In the appointment, the name of Columbus was not even mentioned. This was an open contradiction to the original grant that Columbus had received from the Spanish Royalty. So sweeping were the powers conferred on Bobadilla that Columbus became literally a prisoner of the Governor General. Already by the year 1500, the envy of his enemies became so hostile that Queen Isabella herself, once Columbus' friend, became the tool of his implacable foes. Columbus was summoned to be tried by Bobadilla on charges that history shows were absolutely false. He was put in chains and sent as a prisoner to one of the caravels. The attendants were ordered to bind the Admiral in fetters, but they could not bring themselves to do so. Finally, an impudent and shameless cook by the name of Espinosa, riveted the irons on his master's feet, in the words of a witness, "with the same alacrity and readiness as if he were serving him some savory dish."

This introduction to Columbus' critics was necessary if we are to understand something of the five hundred years of both admiration and animosity associated with the discoverer of the New World. It was not coincidental that when Columbus was put in chains, he was clothed in the robe of St. Francis, and during the whole ordeal behaved as a worthy son of the humble man of Assisi.

As we read through the massive literature on Christopher Columbus, we find especially three charges leveled against his character:

1. He is branded as being an invader of a land that belonged to the gentle inhabitants of the New World.

2. He is charged with being an enslaver of the Indians who, until then, were living in joyful freedom among their contemporaries.

3. Columbus is finally accused of being a cruel oppressor of persons who, until then, had been living in prosperous harmony.

Much has happened since 1892 when the Columbian Exposition was held in Chicago to commemorate the quadric-centennial discovery of America. The Columbian Exposition was held in a generation when Christianity was still strong in North America and the name of Columbus was held in benediction among the followers of Christ.

But now, the media are telling us that the discovery of the New World was cataclysmic.

As a result,

- the influence of Christian Europe rocketed across two continents.

- Christianity became the most powerful religion in the world. It thus became a threat to the non-Christian cultures of Afro-Asia, with its fifteen centuries of belief in the divinity of the Man from Nazareth.

- Native American civilizations collapsed. Their religious beliefs in a plurality of gods were replaced, especially in Latin America, with a rigid monotheism that has survived to the present day.

- Indians died by the millions in a holocaust of new diseases, allegedly imported from Europe.

- Millions of African slaves soon were sailing across the Atlantic. And the slave trade flourished over 300 years.

What, then, is there to commemorate, 500 years after 1492? If the scribes of our age are to be believed, it is the sad tale of those who survived the explosion as two worlds collided: the Christian and the non-Christian; the Christian world imported from Catholic Spain and the non-Christian world of native America before 1492.

Defenders of the Native Indians

A library of literature is in print mourning what happened to the native cultures of North and South America with the landing of Columbus. An earthquake was touched off, we are told. It crushed and all but wiped out many centuries-old civilizations.

Always, the critics concentrate on the unproved 50 million Indian deaths due to the diseases brought in by their European conquerors. Or, the critics point out that America was discovered during the pontificate of Pope Alexander VI, who is described as "probably the most corrupt pontiff in 2000 years of Catholic history" – without distinguishing between Rodrigo Borgia before he became pope and Alexander VI, whose defense of Christian faith and morals was among the most outstanding in Catholic history.

Those who criticize Columbus for destroying, in their words, the precious culture of the American Indians, ignore the grim facts of pre-Columbian American history. A fair example is the Aztec civilization in Mexico. Seemingly advanced in other ways, the Aztec religion sank to some of the worst excesses of superstition. It is so extreme as to be almost incomprehensible to us who are familiar with the barbarous atrocities of the concentration camp and nuclear war.

The Aztec religion sprang from a compulsive instinct to attract those natural forces which were beneficial to man and repel those which were malign. Most of these forces, such as the sun, rain, wind and fire, were personified as gods and goddesses, and idols of these deities were worshipped in the massive pyramidal temples.

The Aztecs felt under a compelling duty to offer human sacrifices to these gods. It was either in atonement for some physical calamity, such as pestilence or earthquake, or to forestall an expected misfortune. The Aztecs felt driven to supply the gods with a regular "nourishment" of human blood for fear that a deity, like the sun, might no longer appear on the eastern horizon.

The victims of these sacrifices were most frequently slaves or prisoners of war. Tearing out the hearts of living victims by black-robed, long-haired, chanting priests was a relatively merciful death compared to being scourged or eaten alive. The killings were on a large scale and would reach thousands on a single day, as failure to influence the gods became a frenzy of slaughter.

Among other historic sources, we have record of what happened at the inauguration in 1487 of the temple of Huitzilopochtli (Wheat zil opochtly), the god of war and of the sun. At the ceremony, some 20,000 human beings were sacrificed on the temple altars at the command of the Aztec Emperor, Auitzotl, to appease the monstrous deity.

When, then, we are told that Columbus destroyed the meek and peace-loving Indian culture, Columbus brought Christianity to the blood-thirsty Indians. Millions embraced the religion of Jesus Christ before the end of the 16th century and became, like the converted Aztec Juan Diego, models of humility and charity.

African Slavery

Among the critics of Columbus, some of the most vociferous are those who charge him with introducing African slavery into the western world.

Totally oblivious of the facts of history, they claim that, shortly after 1492, Columbus ushered in the trans-Atlantic trade in human captives that would enslave 10 million Africans before it was made illegal in the late 1800's. His slanderers further say that Columbus resorted to slavery as his early dreams of riches failed.

What are the facts? We must distinguish between Christopher Columbus himself, and his European contemporaries. No doubt many of the Europeans of the day believed that slavery was morally justified. Columbus himself believed the same. But there is no clear evidence that Columbus approved the enslavement of innocent persons.

Moreover, neither he nor the Europeans introduced slavery into America. It was an established Indian custom for centuries before the discovery of America.

More important, however, is the marked difference between the attitude of the Catholic colonizers of America, like the Spanish and Portuguese, and the attitudes of colonizers from, by then, Protestant countries like England and Holland.

The U.S. had to engage in a civil war to liberate the black slaves by government edict. Three centuries before, however, countries under Catholic influence were already telling their people that slavery was forbidden.

Here the influence of the Popes was paramount. In document after document, the Bishops of Rome protested against the enslavement of the native Indians and the imported Africans. The papal declarations finally prevailed, long before slavery was declared illegal in Anglo-Saxon America.

Appraisal of Christopher Columbus

The real ground for animosity against Columbus is the fact that he brought the Catholic Faith to the New World. Columbus believed he was specially chosen by God to bring the Gospel to a people who were living in darkness and the shadow of death.

His *Book of Prophecies* is a full-scale study of the Messianic prophets of the Old Law and the teaching of Christ about the duty to proclaim the Gospel to all nations.

He was a devout Catholic attending Mass and receiving Holy Communion regularly.

He was a Franciscan Tertiary who believed, like St. Francis, that the world should be converted to Christ by prayer, preaching and peaceful means.

His Journal from August 3 to October 12, 1492 is a daily record of the historic voyage from Spain to the New Indies. Day after day, he refers to Jesus and the need for divine help. He is always asking Our Lord for the light and strength he needs to realize what God had entrusted him to do: the mission of bringing the knowledge and love of Jesus and Mary to the multitudes who had not had the Good News of salvation brought to them.

IV

THE BLESSED VIRGIN MARY AND THE CATHOLIC DISCOVERY OF AMERICA

It must seem strange to associate the Blessed Virgin Mary and the discovery of America.

What makes the subject strange is that most people think of the discovery of the New World in geographic terms. In 1492, an Italian navigator by the name of Christopher Columbus sailed from Spain in search of the Indies and landed in what we now call Central America. His motives, we are told, were economic and psychological. He was looking for the riches of the Orient to extend the political power of the Spanish monarchy. And he sought the very human glory that he was sure to receive once he reached the Far East by going west across the Atlantic.

What most of the English-speaking world does not know is that the dominant motive of Columbus for sailing across the uncharted sea was deeply Catholic. Even more, it was apostolic. As all the primary sources on Columbus make clear, he believed that he was specially chosen by God to extend the Kingdom of Christ to pagan nations who had never had the Gospel preached to them.

If there was one thing that stood out in the Catholic Spain of Columbus' day, it was the people's great devotion to the Blessed Virgin. It was a devotion that took almost eight centuries to mature. How so? Under the heavy pressure of a militant Islam whose basic name in Christianity was idolatry. In the words of the Koran, "the followers of the Nazarene" claimed that His Mother Mary was the Mother of Allah because her Son was the living God who became man for the salvation of the world.

It was not until 1491 that Catholic Spain was liberated from Moslem tyranny. The liberation meant freedom once more to proclaim Mary's divine maternity without fear of Islamic opposition for professing idolatry.

Columbus himself was very devoted to Our Lady. His published writings reveal a childlike dependence on Mary. She was regularly invoked in his prayers. His flagship in crossing the sea was the Santa Maria. And one of the first islands he discovered, he named Concepcion, in honor of Mary's Immaculate Conception.

However, this is not the focus of our lecture on "The Blessed Virgin Mary and the Catholic Discovery of America." Change one word in the title and we have our focus. I wish to speak to you about "The Blessed Virgin Mary and the Catholic Evangelization of America."

It was the apparitions of Our Lady to Juan Diego, the converted Aztec Indian, and her revelations of Guadalupe that opened the greatest missionary expansion of the Gospel since apostolic times.

We shall concentrate on Our Lady of Guadalupe and the conversion of Mexico. But Mexico soon became the inspiration of the rest of Latin America.

Before Guadalupe, 1492 to 1531

In order to appreciate the significance of Mary's role in the conversion of the New World, we must see something of the conditions in Mexico before the events of Guadalupe.

When Columbus crossed the Atlantic, he reached only the outskirts of the Western Hemisphere. He touched on one island after another in the Central American continent. By the beginning of the 1500's, Mexico was discovered. Columbus had already passed to his eternal reward and was followed by one Spanish-appointed governor-general after another.

As we read the history of those early days, we are struck by the stark contrast between Church and state or, more accurately, between men of Christian faith and men of raw human greed and merciless cruelty.

Already among the crew that sailed with Columbus on his first voyage there were kindred spirits with their leader. Like him their dominant motive was to bring the Gospel to the native Indians. But there were also rapacious predators whose one ambition was to accumulate as much gold as possible and subjugate the Indians to virtual or actual slavery.

One name stands out in this period: Cortes was the Spanish general whose military exploits in Mexico rank him with Caesar and Napoleon in his physical conquest of Mexico. As war-like as Cortes was, he was a believing Christian. In the tradition of his ancestors who conquered the Moors in Spain, he wanted Christianity to be established in the lands he conquered. He encouraged the Franciscan missionaries to preach the gospel to the natives.

But Cortes also believed that the Indians should be conquered by force of arms. Thus, he offered truce to the natives of what was then called the City of Mexico. But their emperor, Cuauhtemoc, was persuaded by his pagan priests not to give in to the Christians. In the siege that followed, we are told that 100,000 Indians and their close allies were killed by the sword or by drowning, and as many again who died of starvation, dysentery and other diseases.

Nor was that all. Cortes made some serious blunders as administrator of the Indies. He returned to Spain to defend his reputation and this occasioned Charles V, the Spanish emperor, to send to America two men who were as unlike as day and night. On December 12, 1527, he appointed Franciscan Juan Zumarraga as Bishop-protector of the Indians, and he made the soldier Nuño de Guzman governor of Mexico. The next three years are among the saddest in the history of the New World.

De Guzman not only resented the bishop's role as protector of the Indians. He opposed him and did everything but have him killed. A reign of terror broke out that has no parallel in early American history.

In less than two years at least 10,000 Indians had been shipped to the West Indies to be sold as slaves with no chance of returning to their families. Whole towns were laid waste, priests were kidnapped, flogged and maimed.

These and similar atrocities were reported to Emperor Charles V. In August, 1530, he issued an edict which forbade the enslavement of the Indians. The edict read, "No person shall dare to make a single Indian a slave, whether in war or in peace ...whether by barter, by purchase, by trade, or any other pretext or cause whatever."

Our Lady Appears to Juan Diego

Thus the soil was prepared for sowing the seed of the Gospel and bearing such fruit as has no parallel in the annals of Christianity.

In one short generation, the whole Aztec Empire had undergone a volcanic change. The world in which they had lived for centuries was an evil world in which their gods demanded the killing of thousands of human beings in sacrifice. The Spanish conquistadors had delivered the Indians from pagan tyranny, but also left them dangling without any religious moorings.

If the Indians were to become Christians, they had to see Christianity as something belonging to them. It could not be the religion of foreigners whom they had too often seen as invaders and oppressors.

The man chosen by God to open the most dramatic conversion in Christian misology was himself a convert from paganism.

Born in 1474, he lost his parents in childhood and was brought up by his uncle. On marrying, he settled with his wife at Cuautitlan in a little one-room mud house thatched with corn stalks. In 1525, he was baptized Juan Diego, along with his wife Maria Lucia and his uncle Juan Bernardino. Juan Diego and his wife would frequently walk the fifteen miles to Tlaltelolco, to assist at Mass and receive Holy Communion.

Four years after Baptism, his wife died, leaving him childless. Juan Diego then moved to be closer to his aged uncle, whose house was only nine miles from the nearest Franciscan church.

Juan Diego rose early on the morning of December 9, 1531, which was then the Feast of the Immaculate Conception. The Franciscans were unique in promoting devotion to Mary's Immaculate Conception centuries before the definition of the dogma in 1854.

On his way to Mass, Juan was suddenly stopped by the sound of music at the hill of Tepeyac, the site of the former pagan temple of Tonantzin. He thought it was his imagination, but then saw a glowing white cloud, hallowed by a rainbow formed by streams of lightning coming from the cloud. Then he heard a woman's gentle voice calling out to him in diminutive form, "Juanito...Juan Dieguito."

The Lady asked him where he was going. "I am on my way to the church in Tlaltelolcoto to hear Mass," he told her. The Lady smiled and said, "You must know and be very certain, my son, that I am truly the perpetual and perfect Virgin Mary, Mother of the true God, through Whom everything lives, Who is the Creator and Master of heaven and earth. I ardently desire that a temple be built here in my name where I will show and give all my love, my help and my protection to the people. I am your merciful Mother, the Mother of all who live united in this land, and of all mankind, of all who love me, who cry out to me, and of those who have confidence in me. Here, I will hear their weeping and sorrows, and will remedy and alleviate their sufferings, needs and misfortunes. In order to realize my intentions, go to the house of the Bishop of Mexico City and tell him I sent you and that it is my desire to have a temple built here."

Juan Diego did as the Lady told him to. But Bishop Zumarraga was not impressed. He told the poor Indian to come later at a more convenient time. So Juan returned to the Tepeyac Hill the same evening where the Lady was waiting for him. He urged her to send someone else to the bishop. He himself was a 'nobody' and "I do not want to fall into your displeasure."

But the Lady insisted it must be Juan and he should return to the bishop the next day.

So he came back to the bishop, who this time was more impressed, but also told Juan that the Lady must give some proof that she really is the Mother of God.

Again at sunset, on December 10, a Sunday, he went to Tepeyac, where the Lady appeared to him with the promise that she would provide the miraculous sign requested by the bishop.

At this point there are two versions of what happened. One version has it that when Juan returned home, he found his uncle deathly sick. Another and fully documented version is that his uncle was missing when the nephew returned from Tepeyac Hill. He had been fatally shot by hostile Indians who resented his becoming a Christian and cooperating with the hated Spaniards.

Juan Diego was in a quandary. Should he go back to the bishop as the Lady had instructed him, or should he take care of his uncle? Juan chose to minister to his uncle's desperate needs all day, Sunday, December 11.

Monday morning, December 12, Juan went to get the priest to take care of his dying uncle. In his simplicity, he made a bypass around Tepeyac instead of going to the top of the hill where he was afraid that Our Lady would be waiting for him. But he miscalculated. The Blessed Virgin came down the hill to intercept him. She asked him where he was going. He explained about his uncle.

Then she told him, "Listen and be sure, my dear son, that I will protect you. Do not be afraid nor grieved. Let not your heart be dismayed, no matter how great the illness [of your uncle] of which you speak. I am your mother and is not my help your refuge? Am I not of your kind? Do not be concerned about your uncle's illness. He is not going to die. Be assured he is already well."

Our Lady then told Juan to go to the top of the hill where he would find some flowers which he was to bring to her. The hill was a desert, where only cactus grew. But Juan did as he was told. When he reached the west of the hill, it was covered with beautiful Castilian roses in full bloom. As he later related, Mary took the roses from him as he gathered them and arranged them with her own hands in the cloak or *tilma* that Juan was wearing.

There was one final message from Mary. It is the capstone of Guadalupe and the key to understanding what we are saying when we speak of the Blessed Virgin and the discovery – or conversion – of America: "This is the sign you must take to the Lord Bishop. Tell him in my name that with this he will see and recognize my will. He must do what I ask. You are my ambassador and worthy of my confidence. I counsel you to take every care to speak only in the presence of the Bishop. Tell him what you are carrying and tell him how I asked you to climb the hill to gather the flowers. Also tell him everything you have seen so that you will persuade the Bishop to see that the church I have asked for, will be built."

When Juan reached the Bishop's residence, he was made to wait a long time and the attendants tried to take some of the roses that were in his cloak. But the flowers became like painted embroidery.

On being admitted to Bishop Zumarraga's presence, Diego opened his cloak. Immediately the roses fell in a flood of color to the floor. But that was not all. On the cloak was a portrait of the Mother of God. She was in Indian dress, her hands joined in prayer. Her features were Indian and of startling beauty. Bishop Zumarraga fell to his knees in prayer.

Juan Diego was allowed to retire to a hermitage. He died there in 1548 at the age of 74. He was beatified (1990) and canonized (2002) by (now-Blessed) Pope John Paul II.

The Shrine of Our Lady of Guadalupe

By the end of 1531, the image of Our Lady was exposed in the Bishop's private chapel where it was venerated by thousands of Aztecs. Also before the end of the same year there was a triumphant procession of the sacred image from Mexico City to Tepeyac. On that occasion, a Mexican who had been accidentally killed by an arrow was restored to life.

Since 1531, the Shrine of Our Lady of Guadalupe has become a major basilica. We might say that Mexico City is built around the shrine. But the center remains the image of Our Lady. Its miraculous character has been attested by ecclesiastical, even pontifical, approval. It has also been scientifically examined and proved that the portrait could not have been produced naturally. No painter's brush was used; the tilma is fragile, decay-able cactus fiber. Yet the image remains as clear and fresh as it was almost five centuries ago. Even a terrorist's bomb in 1921 did not scratch the portrait, although it completely bent the metal crucifix next to the image of the Blessed Virgin.

The Miraculous Conversion of Millions

The principal wonder of Guadalupe, however, is not the unexplainable picture of Our Lady. It is not the constant stream of pilgrims to the shrine every year. The real wonder and the main theme of this presentation is the avalanche of conversions which the revelation of Juan Diego began in the Western world.

One historian after another is lost for words to do justice to the phenomenon. In sober fact, it is unprecedented in the twenty centuries of Catholic evangelization.

No sooner had Columbus landed in the West Indies than apostolic men from Spain began to proclaim the Gospel to the natives. Compared with militant conquerors like Cortes and Guzman, the missionaries were mild and gentle apostles of the Word. They devoted themselves ardently to the conversion of the Indians.

But these courageous priests and religious were few in number. The language barrier was practically insurmountable. The number of dialects was innumerable. The territories to be covered were unimaginable. The injustices perpetrated by some of the conquistadors could be indescribable.

No one questions the heroism of these pioneers of Christianity in North and South America. In spite of their gigantic zeal the results were sparse and the number of converts very few.

Here let me quote from one of the leading historiographers of Latin America:

> *Scarcely had the most holy Virgin of Guadalupe appeared and taken possession of this, her inheritance, when the Catholic faith spread with the rapidity of light from the rising sun through the wide extent and beyond the bounds of the ancient empire of Mexico.*
>
> *Countless multitudes from every tribe, every district, every race*

> ...*who were grossly superstitious, who were ruled by the instincts of cruelty, oppressed by every form of violence and utterly degraded, were radically changed once they learned about the marvelous apparitions of Our Lady of Guadalupe. They came to recognize their natural dignity, forgot their misfortunes and put off their impulsive ferocity.*

These pagans, we are told, could not resist the loving invitation of the Mother of God. They flocked in droves to the waters of Baptism, on a scale and with a speed that has no equal in recorded Catholic history.

The missionaries were understandably overwhelmed by the endless crowds who clamored for instruction and Baptism. We have evidence of a single priest administering the Sacrament of Baptism to six-thousand people in a single day.

Wherever the missionaries traveled, entire families would come running out of their poor villages, begging with signs to have the waters of Baptism poured over them.

Along with Baptism the natives were instructed in the basics of Christianity. Nor was that all. Soon churches, monasteries, convents, hospitals, schools and workshops were built to provide for the development and practice of the Catholic faith.

What were the results? Astounding! By 1540, over eight million Aztec Indians had embraced Catholic Christianity.

But that was not all. It would be a mistake to suppose that those were only superficial conversions. In 1552, the University of Mexico was founded on an equal academic footing as the University of Salamanca in Spain.

Before long, Catholic Mexico was sending native-born missionaries to distant lands.

The evangelization of the rest of Latin America is a story of God's grace all by itself. The roots of this evangelization can be mysteriously but legitimately traced to the three memorable days at Guadalupe in 1521.

So true is this that in 1910 Pope St. Pius X proclaimed *Our Lady of Guadalupe* the Patroness of all Latin America. All papal documents since then re-confirm this Marian patronage.

The Holy Father, Blessed Pope John Paul II, (died April 2, 2005 at age 84) made a pilgrimage to the Shrine of Our Lady of Guadalupe in 1979. He composed a prayer on that occasion which it is worth quoting in full. In effect, He was asking Our Lady, Mother of the Americas, to intercede with her Divine Son for the people of the Western World. It was through her that the true faith was miraculously planted in this then-new world. It will also be through her that, 500 years later, there will be, where needed, a reconversion of this people of North and South America.

> *O Immaculate Virgin Mother of the true God and Mother of the Church! You, who from this place reveal your clemency and your pity to all those who ask for your protection, hear the prayer that we address to you with filial trust, and present it to your Son Jesus, our sole Redeemer. Mother of mercy, teacher of hidden and silent sacrifice, to you, who come to meet us sinners, we dedicate on this day all our being and all our love. We also dedicate to you our life, our work, our joys, our infirmities and our sorrows. Grant peace, justice and prosperity to our peoples, for we entrust to your care, Our Lady and our Mother, all that we have and all that we are. We wish to be entirely yours and to walk with you along the way of complete faithfulness to Jesus Christ in His Church: hold us always with your loving hand.*
>
> *Virgin of Guadalupe, Mother of the Americas, we pray to you for all the Bishops, that they may lead the faithful along the paths of intense Christian life, of love and humble service of God and souls. Contemplate this immense harvest and intercede with the Lord that He may instill a hunger for holiness in the whole people of God, and grant abundant vocations of priests and religious, strong in the faith, and zealous dispensers of God's mysteries. Grant to our homes the grace of loving and respecting life in its beginnings, with the same love with which you conceived in your womb the life of the Son of God.*
>
> *Blessed Virgin Mary, Mother of Fair Love, protect our families so that they may always be united and bless the upbringing of our children. Our Hope, look upon us with compassion, teach us to go continually to Jesus and, if we fall, help us to rise again to return to Him by means of the confession of our faults and sins in the Sacrament of Penance, which gives peace to the soul. We beg you to grant us a great love for all the holy Sacraments, which are, as it were, the signs that your Son left on earth.*

Thus, Most Holy Mother, with the peace of God in our conscience, with our hearts free from evil and hatred, we will be able to bring to all true joy and true peace, which come to us from your Son our Lord Jesus Christ, with God the Father and the Holy Spirit, Who lives and reigns for ever and ever. Amen.

V
THE POPES AND THE CATHOLIC DISCOVERY OF AMERICA

This must be the strangest title for a lecture, "The Popes and the Catholic Discovery of America." What makes it strange is that for many people, the last terms they would associate are "Popes" and "America." Not only that, but the last ideas they even want to conceive is the "papacy" having anything to do with "independent" nations like the United States of America.

Yet, the facts of history show that the Bishops of Rome had far more to do with the New World discovered by Columbus than most people realize.

My plan is to address myself to a series of topics, all bearing on the subject of "The Popes and the Catholic Discovery of America."

1. Centuries of Spanish loyalty to the Pope in preparation for Columbus.

2. Catholic evangelization of the New World with massive defection from the papacy in the Old World.

3. Pontifical America, or papal direction and legislation for America in the sixteenth century.

Papal Loyalty in Pre-Columbian Spain

There is more than academic value in at least briefly reviewing Spanish fidelity to the Bishop of Rome before Columbus left Spain to discover the Indies. Why is this important? It is important because it helps to explain why, of all countries, Spain should have been the one to send Columbus to find the Indies.

All the evidence available indicates that what we have come to call the Western Hemisphere had been known to Europeans and Orientals long before Columbus sailed across the Atlantic in 1492. It must have been known. Why? Because the natives of North and South America were themselves immigrants from the Far and Near East. Yet, in the mysterious designs of Providence it was not until the end of the fifteenth century that the so-called New World was "discovered." Equally mysterious is that it should have been Spain to make the discovery. Why Spain?

Many historical or sociological reasons could be given. But they pale into insignificance when compared with one profound theological reason: Spain, at the close of the fifteenth century, was the most "papist" country in the world. Her political rulers were dedicated to the Bishop of Rome. With all their human failings, they recognized the authority of the pope even in matters that today would seem to be outside of papal jurisdiction.

It is not enough to say that this belonged to the Spanish temperament. Nor is it sufficient to say that seven-plus centuries of resisting Moslem oppression had made the Spaniards psychologically conditioned to pontifical loyalty.

No doubt the Spaniards were supported in their conflict with the Moors by the strong encouragement of the popes. But this encouragement would have been meaningless unless the Spaniards deeply believed in the Roman primacy.

Nowhere is this more clearly seen than in the teaching and writing of the Spaniard, St. Ignatius Loyola. He was born in 1491, the very year that Spain was finally liberated from the Moors. So devoted was Ignatius to the papacy that he prescribed on his followers in the Society of Jesus, unconditional obedience to the Bishop of Rome. To this end, he imposed on all professed members of the Society a fourth special vow of obedience to the Pope.

In his classic Letter on Obedience, Ignatius writes: *Divine Providence gently disposes all things, bringing to their appointed end the lowest by the middlemost and the middlemost by the highest. Even in the angels there is subordination of one hierarchy to another ... We see the same on earth in well-governed states, and in the hierarchy of the Church, the members of which render their obedience to the one universal Vicar of Christ Our Lord.*

This attitude of reliance on the pope was built into the Spanish culture. Even when Spaniards failed in their obedience to the pope, they still recognize it was a failure in faith.

The Papacy Abandoned and Discovered

Nothing ever happens by chance. It was, therefore, certainly providential that the massive rejection of the papacy in Europe was countered by a miraculous Catholicism in the New World.

Some dates here will be informative.

- Martin Luther, the founder of Protestantism, was born in 1483, just nine years before Columbus discovered America. Luther's break with the Catholic Church can be synthesized in his rejecting the divinely established authority of the Bishop of Rome.

- Luther broke with Rome in 1517, and he spent the rest of his life in venting his hatred of the papacy. His last published work (1545), was also his bitterest attack on the very institution of supreme Roman authority in the Church founded by Christ. For Luther, the papacy was instituted by the devil.

- In 1535, St. John Fisher was beheaded by Henry VIII because the king insisted that he, and not the Bishop of Rome, was the real head of the Church in England.

- Again, not coincidentally, the Queen of England whom Henry VIII repudiated in favor of his mistress, was the daughter of Queen Isabella of Spain, who sent Columbus on his historic discovery of America. It was, in fact, Catherine of Aragon's appeal to the Pope in favor of her marriage to Henry VIII that precipitated the crisis which separated England from union with the Bishop of Rome.

By the end of the sixteenth century, six whole countries in Europe had separated from the Pope and therefore from the Catholic Church. Under coercion from their political leaders, all of Norway, Sweden, Denmark, England, Scotland and Wales broke with Rome. At the same time, large parts of Germany and Switzerland were either forced or seduced into rejecting "Babylon," which had become the Protestant synonym for the successor of St. Peter.

The Catholic Church in the sixteenth century had desperate need of reformation. Unlike the nations that made this into a rebellion against the papacy, Spain became the spearhead for an authentic Catholic Reform in union with the Pope.

The Catholic Reform Movement became a European movement when Catholic Spain placed all its resources at the service of the Church. The long struggle with Islam closed with the victory at Granada in 1491. Columbus' discovery in the next year opened the door to making Spain a world power that was of paramount importance in the history of the Catholic Church. When the Protestant revolt in Germany was brought to a halt, this was due in large measure to Catholic Spain.

Spain was the cradle of the religious order which became the chief instrument of reform. The key to this reform was faith in the Roman Primacy. Pope Leo X, who condemned Luther, was not personally a very holy man. But the Catholic Church believes that papal authority finally rests on the supernatural grace provided by Jesus Christ. It is not conditioned by the sanctity of Peter's successors in the papacy.

As we cross the Atlantic during the historic upheaval in Europe, we see nothing less than a series of miracles of conversion among the Indians of North and South America. The number of these conversions to Catholic Christianity is staggering. By the middle of the sixteenth century, no less than ten million American Indians had been instructed, baptized and received into the Catholic Church. In 1552, the University of Mexico was opened with papal approval and with academic qualifications that soon compared favorably with the great Catholic universities of Spain and Portugal.

Pontifical America

In 1991, the Pontifical Committee of Historical Services published a two-volume work called *America Pontifica*. The English title would be *Pontifical America*. Its purpose was to bring to light what most people do not know; namely, how deeply and intimately the Bishops of Rome were associated with the founding of the New World.

By no means exhaustive, no less than 579 papal documents are given, in full quotation. These documents cover only the first one hundred years, from 1493 to 1592, after the discovery of America. They amount to some 700,000 words. Every reigning Roman Pontiff from Alexander VI to Clement VIII is included.

As you read these papal documents, all in Latin, you are struck by a number of facts. Taken together they not only justify the title, *Pontifi-*

cal America. They prove beyond doubt that, except for the popes, there would not have been what we casually call the discovery of America. Why not? Because it was the Roman Catholic faith of the first colonizers that laid the foundations for what is known as North and South America.

What are some of the main features of these papal documents?

1. *Propagation of the True Faith.* Beginning with Alexander VI, the popes keep insisting on the importance of propagating the one true Faith. It must be the Faith revealed by Jesus Christ, committed to the Apostles, and preserved in its integrity by the successors of St. Peter.

   This faith must be preserved in its integrity. This means that bishops, priests and lay missionaries are to make sure there is no compromise with the non-Christian religions which the natives had professed for centuries before they were evangelized.

   Among the truths of the faith which the Popes stressed were:

   - Belief in only one true God, Creator of Heaven and earth.

   - Belief in the Incarnation. God became Man; He was conceived by the Holy Spirit in the womb of the Virgin Mary.

   - Belief in the sacraments instituted by Christ. Specially emphasized was the Sacrament of Matrimony for the baptized and the indissolubility of Sacramental Marriage.

2. *Emphasis on the Teachings of the Council of Trent.* As we know, the Council of Trent was called in order to cope with the flood of errors propagated by the leaders of Protestantism. The Council lasted from 1546 to 1563, the longest in the Church's history.

   This stress on Tridentine doctrine was providential. Before long, the European Catholics who had become Protestants – or their descendants – began to colonize on their own. Their colonization became Protestant (and therefore anti-papal) evangelization. The Protestants from England, Scandinavia and the Netherlands mainly settled in North America. Our own experience in the United States shows how deeply Protestant colonization had penetrated our culture, compared with what we still call Latin America.

3. *Religious Countries.* One of the remarkable aspects of the papal documents to the New World is the encouragement of what we now call consecrated life. By the end of the sixteenth century, no less than seventeen different religious orders were established under the direction of the Holy See.

4. *Dioceses and Directives to Bishops.* The Catholic faith spread throughout the Americas, the popes created scores of dioceses, with resident bishops. The papal documents on this subject are extensive and detailed.

One thing stands out, however. The Roman Pontiffs made it clear that the bishops were finally responsible to the Bishop of Rome. When we realize that this was the 16th century, with communications being so difficult, we are struck by the awareness on both sides – the papal and the episcopal – that the Catholic Church has only one central authority, namely the successors of St. Peter.

5. *One of the surprises is that the popes insisted on Ad Limina visits of the bishops to Rome.* The prelates were to report to the Pontiff on their dioceses and make periodic trips to Rome. This could mean as much as two months sea travel, one way, in crossing the Atlantic.

6. *Devotion to the Blessed Virgin Mary.* One prominent theme that typifies the pope's directives to the New World is the insistence on a strong devotion to the Blessed Virgin Mary.

No less than 14 distinct Marian Associations were established by papal decree or pontifical directive. The focus of these associations, called Confraternities, was to help the people to depend on Our Lady to keep them faithful to her Divine Son. This was especially true after the revelations of

Our Lady of Guadalupe to Juan Diego, the Aztec convert, in 1531.

Epilogue

What can we learn from our reflections on "The Popes and the Catholic Discovery of America." Many things, but especially one: that the future of both continents of the Western World is secure, provided we rely on the Mother of God to obtain the miraculous graces we need to remain true to our Catholic heritage.

Closing Prayer

"O Immaculate Virgin Mother of the true God and Mother of the Church! You, who from this place reveal your clemency and your pity to all those who ask for your protection, hear the prayer that we address to you with filial trust and present it to your Son Jesus, our sole Redeemer. Mother of mercy, teacher of hidden and silent sacrifice, to you who come to meet us sinners, we dedicate on this day all our being and all our love. We also dedicate to you our life, our work, our joys, our infirmities and our sorrows. Grant peace, justice and prosperity to our peoples, for we entrust to your care, Our Lady and our Mother, all that we have and all that we are. We wish to be entirely yours and to walk with you along the way of complete faithfulness to Jesus Christ in His Church: hold us always with your loving hand."

"Virgin of Guadalupe, Mother of the Americas, we pray to you for all the Bishops, that they may lead the faithful along the paths of intense Christian life, of love and humble service of God and souls. Contemplate this immense harvest, and intercede with the Lord that He may instill a hunger for holiness in the whole People of God, and grant abundant vocations of priests and religious, strong in the faith and zealous dispensers of God's mysteries. Grant to our homes, the grace of loving and respecting life in its beginnings with the same love with which you conceived in your womb the life of the Son of God."

"Blessed Virgin Mary, Mother of Fair Love, protect our families so that they may always be united and bless the upbringing of our children.

Our Hope, look upon us with compassion, teach us to go continually to Jesus and, if we fall, help us to rise again, to return to Him by means of the confession of our faults and sins in the Sacrament of Penance, which gives peace to the soul. We beg you to grant us a great love for all the holy Sacraments, which are, as it were, the signs that your Son left on earth. Thus, Most Holy Mother, with the peace of God in our conscience, with our hearts free from evil and hatred, we will be able to bring to all true joy and true peace, which come to us from your Son, our Lord Jesus Christ, Who with God the Father and the Holy Spirit, lives and reigns for ever and ever. Amen."

VI

FIVE HUNDRED YEARS SINCE COLUMBUS ~ LESSONS OF THE CHURCH'S HISTORY

Our reflections so far on Christopher Columbus have concentrated on his Catholic discovery of America. Our stress has been on the providential role that Columbus played in initiating the most fruitful conversion to Catholic Christianity since apostolic times.

In this closing chapter we shall cover, in cameo, the five hundred years since Columbus landed in America. We hope to see what have been the outstanding features of the Church's history in the New World in the past half millennium. Even more pertinently, we will ask ourselves: What lessons does the Church's experience teach us today, as we begin the next five hundred years of Catholic history in the New World.

Inevitably, we shall have to be very selective. Too much has happened since 1492 and no two evaluations will be the same. However, there are certain aspects of our Catholic history since Columbus that are too obvious to be missed. They are also too important not to learn from the past how God wants us Catholics to live the future in a world that, by His standards, is only a half-day old. If ever the proverb was true that "Those who ignore history will have to relive it," it is painfully true for us Catholics as we face the twenty-first century in the Western Hemisphere.

What are we saying? We are saying that Catholic Christianity is faced with a resurgent paganism in the two Americas. No less than the America discovered by Columbus had to be evangelized, America today has to be re-evangelized. No less than the Native Americans of the late fifteenth century had to be converted to Jesus Christ and His humanly impossible demands on fallen human nature, so the America of the late twentieth century must be reconverted to the teachings of the Divine Master. But there is one big difference. The Aztecs and Mohawks and Chippewas of Columbus' time had not ever been Christian. They had never been touched by the Gospel. Their conversion, therefore, required only the abandonment of their non-Christian way of life. However, to give our secularized Americans a new name, the Aztecs and Mohawks and Chippewas of our day have to be converted twice over:

- Their *minds* must be converted in humble submission to the teaching of Christ which so many have rejected because they have become "too educated" to accept, as they say, childish dogmas of a pre-scientific age.

- Even more difficult, their *wills* have to be converted to obey what the Church teaches are divine imperatives but which so many modern philosophies dismiss as out-dated fanaticism.

Any one of these lessons of Catholic history since Columbus deserves a volume of commentary. We shall limit ourselves to only a few salient observations on each of the instructive features of the Church's history since Columbus left Catholic Spain and reached what he called San Salvador in 1492.

Missionary Zeal

As we have seen, the underlying drive that led Columbus to discover what turned out to be a new world was his passionate desire to bring the Good News of the gospel to the non-Christian peoples of what he had first thought was the Far East. This motivation sustained him and was shared not only by Queen Isabella of Spain. It was the dominant reason why Pope Alexander VI spoke of Columbus as "our beloved son" because he had opened the door to the evangelization of millions who until then were deprived of the Light of the World. It was the underlying factor which sent shiploads of missionaries to bring God's revealed word to the teeming millions of American polytheists. The following quotation is quite lengthy. But it deserves to be given, in full. It is from the document of Pope Paul III, dated June 2, 1537, in which the Bishop of Rome defends the native Indians against the charge that they are too ignorant to be taught the Christian faith. It is, however, more than a defense of the native intelligence of the Indians and their capacity to be Christianized. It is a Magna Charta for what became the Church's vision of a whole new world being brought to the Heart of Christ.

> *The sublime God so loved the human race that He created man in such wise that he might participate, not only in the good that other creatures enjoy, but endowed him with capacity to*

attain to the inaccessible and invisible Supreme Good and behold It face to face; and since man, according to the testimony of the Sacred Scriptures, has been created to enjoy eternal life and happiness, which none may obtain save through faith in our Lord Jesus Christ, it is necessary that he should possess the nature and faculties enabling him to receive that faith; and that whoever is thus endowed should be capable of receiving that same faith. Nor is it credible that any one should possess so little understanding as to desire the faith and yet be destitute of the most necessary faculty to enable him to receive it. Hence Christ, who is the Truth Itself that has never failed and can never fail, said to the preachers of the faith whom He chose for that office, "Go, ye, and teach all nations." He said all, without exception, for all are capable of receiving the doctrines of the faith.

The enemy of the human race who opposes all good deeds in order to bring men to destruction, beholding and envying this, invented a means never before heard of, by which he might hinder the preaching of God's word of salvation to the people. He inspired his satellites who, to please him, have not hesitated to publish abroad that the Indians of the west and the south and other people of whom we have recent knowledge, should be treated as dumb brutes created for our service, pretending that they are incapable of receiving the Catholic Faith.

We who, though unworthy, exercise on earth the power of our Lord and seek with all our might to bring those sheep of his flock who are outside, into the fold committed to our charge, consider, however, that the Indians are truly men and that they are not only capable of understanding the Catholic faith but according to our information, they desire exceedingly to receive it.

By virtue of our apostolic authority we define and declare that the said Indians and other peoples should be converted to the faith of Jesus Christ by preaching the word of God and by the example of good and holy living.

Nothing could be clearer than the teaching of the Pope that the Native Indians were fully qualified to embrace the Catholic faith. What may not be so obvious is that the Spanish, Portuguese and French colonizers had a very low estimate of the intelligence and moral character necessary for conversion. This was in stark contrast to the later colonizers from the by then non-Catholic countries like England, the Netherlands and Scandinavia. Spain, Portugal and France had their share of cruel and immoral citizens. But they were then still Catholic countries and the voice of the Bishop of Rome was a directive from the Vicar of Christ. In the same document quoted above, Pope Paul III warned his Catholic subjects not to oppress the Indians. He formally commanded that the Indians "are by no means to be deprived of their liberty or the possession of their property." He forbade that "they be in any way enslaved." The reason for this injunction was not only because to act otherwise would be a grave sin against justice. It would also deprive and, with emphasis, deprive the Indians, of their strongest motive for accepting the teachings of Christ; namely, the witness of the love of Christ practiced by the Christians who had politically conquered the Native Americans.

There is more here than you will ever find in most books on the history of post-Columbian America. The Christian charity demanded of the Catholic colonizers was, we may say, the single most effective factor in their successful missionary zeal. This stands in sharp contrast to the hundreds of thousands of American natives who never accepted the Gospel where the fullness of Catholic truth was not made available and was not combined with the selfless Christian charity. It was the charity demanded by the popes of their Catholic subjects who were so naturally tempted to subject the Indians to political control and even open slavery.

What is the lesson for us in our day? It is very plain. Believing Catholics are to exercise uncommon zeal in favor of their non-Catholic or ex-Catholic or anti-Catholic contemporaries. This zeal must be combined with a deep love for those who do not share our true Faith or who abandoned it, or who are hostile to what the Church teaches the whole world is the will of God. Catholic orthodoxy here is not enough. Orthodoxy without charity is not Christianity. It will require heroic effort on our part to love those who do not love what we believe and may even hate us for living our faith.

The Witness of Martyrdom

The Fathers of the Church had a saying which has become standard in Catholic history. They declared, *"the blood of martyrs is the seed of Christians."* Christianity was born in the Roman Empire; it grew and flourished because Christians were so ready to shed their blood with Christ for the propagation of the Church which was born on Calvary. This has been the law of supernatural propagation ever since.

No history of Western Christianity in the past five centuries would be complete without recognizing this law of spiritual re-productivity in practice. From the earliest days of American colonization, the soil of the New World was nourished by the blood of martyrs.

During the three centuries between the entrance of the first priests into Florida in the early 1520's and the founding of the last California missions in 1823, hundreds of Catholic missionaries labored in every part of what is now the United States. They had one towering aim: to convert the native Indians to Catholic Christianity. Their efforts were remarkably successful, but only at the price of the lives of many of these heralds of the Gospel.

In 1540, Coronado made a historic expedition from Mexico to what is now Florida. He was accompanied by three Franciscan friars. When Coronado turned back in disappointment in the spring of 1542, the friars stayed behind to evangelize the Indians. Soon after, one of them, Fr. Juan de Padilla, was murdered by the red men and thus became the first martyr of the future United States. We do not know what happened to the other two Franciscans except that they disappeared from sight and were never heard from again. We are certain, however, that Juan de Padilla was killed for the Faith. One of Coronado's soldiers, who testified to Padilla's martyrdom, described him as "a man of good and holy life."

The martyrology of North and South America in the past five centuries is a library of men, women and children who shed their blood for Christ and His Church. The North American Jesuit martyrs have all been canonized. What is not common knowledge is that six of them were priests and two were lay missionaries. Saints Isaac Jogues, Anthony Daniel, John de Brebeuf, Gabriel Lalemant, Charles Garnier, Noel Chabanel (priests) and Rene Groupil and John LaLande (lay missionaries) were martyred between September 29, 1642 and December 9, 1649 in the Missions of New France. They were canonized by Pope Pius XI on June 29, 1930.

So the litany of North and South American evangelization could go one. Only God knows the number of these martyrs, as only He knows what courage He inspired in them to remain faithful to the Christ in Whom they believed. The biographies of these witnesses to the True Faith are practically unknown. What we do know is that missionaries and converts suffered unspeakably. Just one example of how the Iroquois dealt with the priest John de Brebeuf and the lay catechist Gabriel Lalemant. Both were led to two posts which were to be their crosses of martyrdom. They knelt down and grasped the posts and prayed to God while Indians stabbed them with sharp instruments. They heated a half a dozen iron hatchets until they were red hot and made a necklace of these blazing hatchets which they placed on Brebeuf's shoulders. Because he kept silence, the savages were irritated at his not pleading for mercy. Brebeuf encouraged the Catholic Christians, telling them "Let us lift our eyes to heaven at the height of our afflictions; let us remember that God is the witness of our suffering, and He will soon be our exceeding great reward." To keep him silent, the barbarians cut off his nose, tore off his lips and gagged his mouth by forcing a hot iron down his throat. In imitation of Baptism, they poured several kettles of scalding water over his head. One Indian scalped him; another cut off his feet; and still others sliced strips of his seared flesh and ate them as he continued praying for his tormentors. Finally, someone buried a hatchet in his jaw and severed it from his face. Then an Iroquois pounced on his body and cut open his breast to get at his heart which the Indians then proceeded to eat because they believed this would give them a share in his indomitable courage.

It was worth going through these details, which could be duplicated many times over the centuries that Christianity was gradually penetrating the pagan world of the Americas.

Again, the lesson for us. From Good Friday on, the teaching of Christ has met with two different kinds of response. Some believed in Christ but most of his own contemporaries did not. Yet they not only rejected His teaching. They persecuted Him and finally crucified Him as a blasphemer and enemy of the people. This has been the pattern ever since. A surprising number of natives accepted the Gospel and became faithful Christians. But many did not. The Christian martyrs of the New World were simply carrying on where Christ had begun. His death on the Cross has ever since been the price of those who carry out His commission to preach the Gospel to all nations.

Although we have already alluded to this, something more should be said here about the difference between the evangelization in what we now call North and South America. North America, above the Rio Grande, had been early penetrated by Europeans who by then had either rejected the Catholic Faith or were the descendants of those who broke with the Church of Rome. Objective historians of North American history are unsparing in their comparison between the way the Natives were treated by colonizers from Catholic countries and by those from countries that had abandoned the Catholic faith. Just one general observation can be made. In areas where the Catholic faith still dominated the colonial powers, the native Indians were treated with relative justice and charity. The injunctions and excommunications of one Pope after another controlled the natural selfish instincts of the European "conquerors." Without obedience to this authority and deprived of the sacraments available to believing Catholics, the colonizers would become just that: colonizers. Their interest was to acquire and dominate and exploit, and the American natives were the logical, even though unwilling, victims of this "colonization."

When, then, we speak of martyrdom as one of the features of the Catholic discovery and conversion of America, we are saying much more than most people realize. Martyrdom is not an isolated phenomenon that characterizes the original evangelization of a pagan culture to authentic Christianity. It is what the Catholic Church experienced when the true Gospel was first preached to the polytheists of Columbian America, has been the continuing experience of every believing Catholic who is loyal to the teaching and example of Jesus Christ. We said that the blood of martyrs is the seed of the Church. But let us be clear as to what we are saying. The blood of martyrs is the constant seed of the Church. A farmer does not sow the seed of his crop only once and then the crop spontaneously grows without repeated plowing and sowing and harvesting year after year. The same holds true for the Church which Christ founded. Its seed must be sown frequently, even regularly, to ensure a constant harvest. Once we say this, it becomes clear that the Church needs martyrs constantly if, in a familiar phrase, the seed of Christians is to produce the spiritual harvest that Christ expects of His followers.

It takes no St. Paul to tell us that the New World to which Columbus brought the True Faith has fallen into the old paganism of the Roman Empire at the dawn of Christianity. If the Church needed martyrs in the age of Nero, Decius and Diocletian (Roman Emperors and persecutors of Christians), she needs martyrs more than ever in our day.

Conformism

Running through the sixteenth century papal documents to the bishops of South America, the Popes keep warning them not to allow their native converts to conform to the pagan practices of their former polytheism. With a wisdom that goes back to the Gospels, the Bishops of Rome could distinguish between the essentials of Christianity and the accidentals of paganism. Christianity believes in only one infinite God Who is the Creator of heaven and earth. Paganism believes in a plurality of deities, both good and bad, who demand recognition and veneration. Christianity believes in the Ten Commandments and their elevation by Christ as spelled out in the Sermon on the Mount. Paganism is, at root, self-centered and, in spite of its polytheism, finally rests on the deification of self. Christianity believes that our lives here on earth are only a prelude and preparation for eternal life in the world to come. Paganism is, to say the least, very confused about the purpose of our existence on earth and even more confused about man's eternal destiny. Catholic Christianity believes in the sacraments and the Real Presence of Christ in the Holy Eucharist, in the Sacrament of Penance, in the Sacrament of Matrimony which unites a man and woman to a lifelong commitment to selfless love. Christianity believes that God became man in the Person of Jesus Christ, Who founded the Church which is the Mother and Teacher of the human race, with a visible head on earth who has supreme authority over the people of God. Catholic Christianity finally believes that Christ instituted the Sacrament of the Priesthood which has power from Him to change bread and wine into the Incarnate Son of God and to reconcile sinners with their offended Master and Lord.

Parallel with these beliefs of those who profess the Catholic Faith, pagans in every age and in every place do not believe what the Church founded by Christ is convinced are divinely revealed truths and norms of human morality.

What the popes told the early American converts from Indian mythology, they have not ceased telling professed Catholics in the New World for the last five hundred years. However, a new dimension has entered American history since the sixteenth century. The new dimension is the New Christianity that was born in sixteenth century Europe with the rise of Luther and Calvin, Zwingli and Cranmer and their transfer of authority from the Church under the Pope, to the state under the king, or parliament or Congress or, as in the United States, the Supreme Court.

Already in the Gospels, Christ warned His followers not to be conformed to the world whose prince, He said, is the devil. The pressure to conformity to the world of our day is greater than it ever was in the first century after the discovery of America. History would bear out the following conclusion: The Catholic Faith brought to the western world by Christopher Columbus has flourished in the exact measure that professed Catholics have resisted conforming themselves to the secular world of their day. Paganism and polytheism are not limited to any particular era or culture. They are as universal as human nature and are only as controlled as the Catholic Church is strong in her resistance to the power of the secularized society in which her members live.

There is a close connection between martyrdom and the conformism of which we are now speaking. It takes heroic strength to witness to Christ, even unto death, in a world that is naturally hostile to Jesus Christ. Another name for this heroism is martyrdom. What the first generations of Christians in America should teach us is that, like them, we must be willing even to die for our Catholic convictions if we are to be conformed to Jesus Christ and not be conformed to the world which crucified Him.

Marital Stability and Morality

The people of the Western Hemisphere in 1492 were natural in the plainest sense of the word. Their fallen human nature was notorious. All the premises of Christ's teaching on marriage were contradicted by the natives that Columbus found in Central America. Nor were the practices of the Native Indians much different anywhere else in the Americas. Polygamy was commonplace. Incest was often a law of life for the survival of an Indian tribe. With the prevalence of slavery, it was assumed that wives became the property of those who had conquered their tribal enemies. One historian after another, in describing the dress and behavioral pattern of the Native Americans leaves no doubt that Christian chastity was an innovation in the society that Columbus found.

As you read the story of the widespread conversion of the natives to Christianity in sixteenth century America, you are struck by its remarkable similarity to the rise of Christianity in the first three centuries after Christ. What especially attracted the pagans of Rome was the example of chastity and charity by the believing Christians. These two virtues were always seen together. They were especially remarkable among the unmarried who preserved their chastity and some even died in defense of their virginity. Among the married, the pagans were struck by the Christian commitment to a lifetime fidelity of the spouses to each other and their absolute rejection of contraception, abortion and infanticide that were the rule in the non-Christian Roman Empire.

An exact parallel to this phenomenon was the dramatic change in morals among the Christian converts after the evangelization which followed on Columbus' discovery of the Indies. One Papal document after another to the bishops of the New World in the sixteenth and seventeenth centuries assumes that those who had embraced Christianity were also living their Christian faith, especially in their practice of chastity and marital morality. A classic example of the spiritual heights that the former pagans could reach is the story of Kateri Tekakwitha. Born in what is now Auriesville, New York in 1656 (?), she died in Southern Canada in 1680. Her mother was a Christian Algonquin who was taken captive by the Iroquois and made the wife of a pagan chief of the Mohawk tribe. Tekakwitha was one of two children born of this coerced marriage. At the age of four, the girl was taken into the home of an uncle after she lost her father, mother and brother in a smallpox epidemic. The disease left her disfigured and with impaired eyesight. In 1667, she met her first Christian missionaries. But fear of her uncle kept her from taking instructions. Finally, in 1675 she was instructed in the Catholic Faith and baptized on Easter Sunday 1676. She took the name of Kateri or Katherine. Her conversion and virtuous life stirred up so much opposition that she had to flee for her life to a Christian Indian village two hundred miles away. Her life of extraordinary charity was joined with a private vow of chastity which placed her under superhuman pressure from those with whom she lived. She was beatified by Blessed Pope John Paul II in 1980. Her popular name of "Lily of the Mohawks" testifies to her heroic practice of chastity and the influence that her charity had in bringing her fellow Indians to accept the Gospel of Christ.

As we look at our own day, the lesson this should teach us is both sobering and inspiring. It is sobering when we see the dregs of immorality to which so many of our fellow Americans have fallen. It is inspiring because we know that part of the responsibility for the un-chastity and un-charity in our society is due to our failure as Catholics to be the channels of grace to our fellow Americans that Our Lord expects us to be.

Our Responsibility

In closing this final presentation on the Catholic discovery of America, I would like to emphasize the duty we have to rediscover America. What do I mean? I mean that we are extraordinarily privileged to be celebrating the quincentennial of Christopher Columbus's finding the New World exactly 500 years ago.

How are we privileged? We are able to learn from the past half millennium that God has special designs for us Catholics in our day. What are these designs? They are nothing less than the purpose that God had in sending Columbus to pagan America. It was to bring Christ and His teaching, to bring the Church and her sacraments, to the polytheists who had never even heard the names of Jesus and Mary.

But in 500 years, Christianity in the western world needs repair – call it reparation; it needs reform – call it reformation; it needs rebuilding – call it edification.

It is our God-given obligation, as believing and practicing Catholics in America, to not only commemorate the discovery of the New World. We are to cooperate with God in the spiritual rebuilding of our country.

The grace of God is available. What He wants from us is something of the zeal of Columbus to extend the Kingdom of Christ in the hearts of our fellow-Americans. What God wants of us is something of the courage of the martyrs who watered the soil of our country with their blood. Why? That we might be free, in the deepest sense of the word, by possessing the Truth which is Jesus Christ, so that by believing in Him here on earth, we may possess Him as a society in that eternal Kingdom of heaven for which we were made.

A First-hand look...

On his remarkable voyage of discovery, Christopher Columbus kept a detailed, day by day log. Beginning with the prayer, *The Sign of the Cross,* Father Hardon notes, Columbus constantly invokes the name of Christ or Divine Providence. His words of October 12, 1492 are especially revealing in regard to his hopes for the natives he has encountered in this new land.

> "The people here...are friendly and well-dispositioned...who bear no arms except for small spears and they have no iron.
>
> I want the natives to develop a friendly attitude towards us because I know they are a people who can be made free and converted to our Holy Catholic Faith, more by love than by force. I therefore gave red caps to some and glass beads to others.
>
> They hung the beads around their necks...and they took great pleasure in this and became so friendly that it was a marvel.
>
> They traded and gave everything they had with good will, but it seems to me they have very little and are poor in everything.
>
> I warned my men to take nothing from the people without giving something in exchange."

See page 11.

The following prayer was composed by Father Hardon in 1992 and was distributed far and wide to pray for our country and that we elect good, moral leaders.

Quincentennial Election Prayer

Lord Jesus Christ, You told us to give to Caesar what belongs to Caesar, and to God what belongs to God.

Enlighten the minds of our people during this Quincentennial year of the discovery of America. May we choose a President of the United States, and other government officials, according to Your Divine Will.

Give our citizens the courage to choose leaders of our nation who respect the sanctity of unborn human life, the sanctity of the family, and the sanctity of the aging.

Grant us the wisdom to give You, what belongs to You, our God. If we do this as a nation, we are confident You will give us an abundance of Your blessings through our elected leaders.

Amen.

Composed by John A. Hardon, S. J.
Imprimatur: Rene H. Gracida
Bishop of Corpus Christi
July 7, 1992

FR HARDON CATHOLIC PRAYER BOOK
by John A. Hardon, S.J.

#E3510	THE FATHER HARDON CATHOLIC PRAYER BOOK	$13.95
#E3511	PRAYER BOOK (LG PRINT)	$15.95
#E7998	PRAYER BOOK (LG PRINT)W RIBBON	$16.95

463 pp.

The deep spirituality of Father Hardon is evident in this selection of prayers and meditations – a superior compilation of materials that will draw ones heart, mind and soul to God. Father Hardon's Catholic Prayer Book is an outstanding collection of traditional and contemporary prayers and meditations. It is designed to help the Catholic in today's culture, just as in times past, to understand the reason for our existence and to give fitting honor and glory to the One Who is our Creator, Our Lord and Our God. True prayer draws us closer to God. By enlisting the help of Our Blessed Mother and the angels and saints, we develop a spiritual journey through this life leading to Eternal Happiness.

The **leatherette cover** with **gold lettering** makes it a beautiful treasure of excellent quality and workmanship - a beautiful gift!

#E3508	MODERN CATHOLIC DICTIONARY (S)	$15.95
#E3509	MODERN CATHOLIC DICTIONARY (H)	$26.95

635 pp.

Father Hardon's *Modern Catholic Dictionary* (available in both softcover and hardcover) is without equal a handy, definitive reference manual for parents, teachers, students – for everyone. It contains over 5,000 terms dealing with Catholic faith, worship, morals, history and spirituality. It defines Catholic terms in clear, concise, understandable language as only Father Hardon can illustrate. Unbelievably low prices for both hardcover and softcover, make this large resource volume an exceptional buy, very affordable, and a treasured gift. There is also a special reference section containing thirteen categories of useful information. Shrink-wrapped. This small book is a brilliant jewel of hope, inspiration and spiritual growth. Make it a part of your daily routine - you will be forever grateful.

THE BLESSED SACRAMENT

John A. Hardon, S.J.

#E3560 $15.00

Father John Hardon, S.J. at his remarkable best! Transcribed from a series of 12 conferences given by Father Hardon in 1998, this new publication by Father will give you fresh insights and many avenues for meditation on Jesus in His Real, true, physical, spiritual Presence in the Blessed Sacrament—a thorough compendium of what the Church teaches regarding the Holy Eucharist. Are we ready to totally know and love God and rely faithfully on Him to guide us through the trials of our modern world so that we faithfully serve Him?

We better be. Our salvation depends on it.

#E3530 **MEDITATIONS ON THE ANGELS** **$7.95**

153 PP.

    This extraordinary and beautiful treatment of the Church's teaching concerning the angels, their role in Divine Providence, and their continuing activity (most notably in our own time, at Fatima), gives us renewed hope and the encouragement to persevere in resisting the fallen angels – the *demons* – and all those who would put obstacles before us in our struggle to live according to Christ's plan for our redemption and salvation. This illuminating study of the angels is sorely needed in the pagan world in which we now live, in the midst of the confusion and deceit around us. Never has a book such as this been more needed than it is today, to give a clear understanding of the role of angels in Divine Providence, particularly as it relates to each of us in our daily lives.

    The spiritual world has been portrayed at its worst over the past years, with tremendous emphasis on the demonic and the ugly; the results of disobedience to God's Divine Will. It's time to proclaim the joy that comes from knowing that Almighty God created the angelic world in beauty; a world in which we can join the angels in singing *"Holy, Holy, Holy, Lord God of Hosts!"*

    Order several. Just over 150 pages, it is easy to read and gives us insights we have not considered before. In his usual, unique fashion, Father Hardon leads us to a clear understanding of God's remarkable gift to mankind – the Angels.